Witold Koszela

Battleships
Nelson & Rodney

ShipShapes

Published in Poland in 2020
by STRATUS s.j.
Po. Box 123,
27-600 Sandomierz 1, Poland
e-mail: office@mmpbooks.biz
as
MMPBooks,
e-mail: rogerw@mmpbooks.biz
© 2020 MMPBooks.
http://www.mmpbooks.biz

ISBN
978-83-65958-35-8

Editor in chief
Roger Wallsgrove

Editorial Team
Bartłomiej Belcarz
Robert Pęczkowski
Artur Juszczak

Research and Text by
Witold Koszela

Drawings and colour profiles
Witold Koszela

Translation
Kazimierz Zygadło

Proofreading
Mathew Willis

DTP
Stratus sp. j.

Printed by
**Wydawnictwo
Diecezjalne i Drukarnia w Sandomierzu**
www.wds.pl

PRINTED IN POLAND

Battleships *Nelson* and *Rodney*

The British battleships HMS *Nelson* and HMS *Rodney*, commissioned in 1927, were among the most unusual in the history of shipbuilding. Their unconventional profiles with three triple main armament turrets, all on the foredeck, and the massive bridge superstructure towards the stern, guaranteed these ships a special place in history and helped make them the subject of numerous books and articles.

The Washington Treaty, signed in February 1922, aimed to rebalance the number of modern ships among the largest navies of the period, and had a serious impact on the battleship. Almost every larger navy had to scrap a significant number of valuable units and cease the construction of new ones.

The "battleship building holiday", as historians have called the provisions of the aforementioned treaty and its subsequent extension in 1936 London Treaty, resulted in an almost fifteen year period in which the construction of battleships was suspended.

An exception to these provisions was that the Royal Navy was granted permission to build two new battleships designed within strict limits. These did not allow for the construction of any battleship hitherto planned by the Admiralty. It meant that all the previous designs had to be abandoned and new ones had to be developed.

In order to meet the displacement constraints, the ships were designed in a most unusual way. The armament comprised nine 406 mm (16 in) guns mounted in three triple turrets located in the forward section, which meant that one of the turrets was in the so-called super-firing position. The superstructure, power plant, crew compartments,

Nelson at sea. The main battery 'A' and 'B' turrets are clearly visible.

etc. were moved towards the stern. The secondary armament, which comprised twelve 152 mm (6 in) guns, was mounted in twin turrets, as opposed to casemates as in previous British battleship classes.

It was no small revolution in the design of the capital ship, which allowed for a significant reduction in the amount of armour needed to protect the most vital areas, with a beneficial effect on displacement. Moving the propulsion unit towards the stern was also an unusual solution, all the more so in that the engine rooms were placed forward of the boiler rooms.

All these made the ships unique, but opinions about them are divided. While they employed numerous innovative solutions in their construction, making them unique in battleship design, many specialists believe that these ships were only powerful and modern on paper. Criticisms include their slow speed in comparison to battleships built in the 1930s, corresponding more closely to that of World War I warships. Undoubtedly this was one of their most significant shortcomings, but as history, and especially the duel between *Rodney* and the German *Bismarck* has shown, they were valuable units and made no small contribution to the Royal Navy operations during World War II.

Sailors nicknamed the battleships *Nelsol* and *Rodnol* as, with their superstructure carried aft, they bore a superficial resemblance to large fleet tankers, whose names carried the "-ol" suffix.

Launch of the battleship HMS Nelson *at Armstrong Whitworth & Co Ltd. on 3 September, 1925.*

Rodney *in an interesting bow shot at the Cowes anchorage. The main battery turrets and awnings in the vicinity of the superstructure are clearly visible.*

5

General characteristics

Hull and superstructure

The hulls of the battleships *Nelson* and *Rodney* were 216.6 m (710.6 ft) long overall (OA), 201.3 m (660.4 ft) between perpendiculars (BP) and 32.3 m (105.4 ft) on the beam. The shape was characterised by straight cutaway stem, cruiser stern – characteristic of British designs – and straight sides without external anti-torpedo bulges. A flush deck, a solution not used in British battleship design since the Lord Nelson-class pre-dreadnoughts, is also worthy of attention. The flush deck, running along the entire length of the hull, allowed for a convenient arrangement of armament, superstructure and fittings, but also had a serious drawback

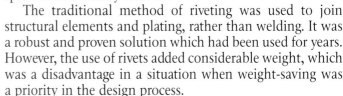

in the form of an insufficient sheer in the forward sections, which, during the service of both ships, manifested itself in flooding of almost all of the bow during cruises at high speed and in stormy weather.

The traditional method of riveting was used to join structural elements and plating, rather than welding. It was a robust and proven solution which had been used for years. However, the use of rivets added considerable weight, which was a disadvantage in a situation when weight-saving was a priority in the design process.

As far as weight savings were concerned, "D" steel, of much higher tensile strength than previously used materials, was used for hull construction in order to remain within the displacement limit. That allowed thinner and thus lighter plates to be used.

In order to provide adequate protection, the hulls of both battleships were divided by transverse bulkheads into 22 watertight compartments. Magazines and boiler rooms also had additional longitudinal bulkheads. (It is interesting to note that, contrary to previous British warships armed with 381 mm/15 in guns, shell rooms were located above the magazines.)

The double bottom compartments were 1.5 m high and ran almost the entire length of the hull. Below the boiler rooms and between bulkheads 172 and 188 they were used as fuel tanks. The remaining fuel tanks were located abreast the magazines, where they would act as additional protection. If necessary, they could be flooded to serve as ballast tanks.

There were five decks: the upper deck, main deck, armoured deck over the machinery and magazines, the middle deck, the lower deck and the platform deck.

One of the most characteristic features of the *Nelson* class battleships was their superstructure. Its location in the stern section was in itself unorthodox, but its design was also quite unusual. In this case British designers decided to move away from the classic solution, which could be observed on previous battleships classes such as the Queen Elizabeth-class and Revenge-class ships, in which the open bridge structure was hung around a heavy tripod foremast. On *Nelson* and *Rodney*, this was replaced with a massive enclosed multi-level bridge structure within which the navigation and signal platforms were included. It was an innovative solution, which offered the crew much better conditions, especially in bad weather. Moreover, the bridge tower served as a solid support for fire control equipment, observation posts, etc.

The ships had a single funnel each, with 36-inch searchlight platforms on both the sides. Two more searchlights were fitted on a tripod mainmast, which also served as a base for the derrick used for handling the ship's boats.

Nelson *leaving Portsmouth. The mast, unnaturally tall in relation to the rest of the superstructure, which was a characteristic feature of both ships in the initial period of their service, is worthy of attention.*

Armour and underwater protection

Nelson and *Rodney* were the first British battleships to embody the "all-or-nothing" armour scheme, which provided protection only to the most vital areas essential for keeping the ship operational. Placement of the main armament turrets forward of the bridge structure played an important role in reducing the size of the armoured citadel and thus also lowering the total weight of the armour. In the case of the Nelson class battleships, the citadel extended for 117 metres, which constituted 58% percent of the ship's length (BP), from the outer face of 'A' barbette to the after bulkhead of the engine room.

The main belt was fitted internally at an angle of 18° to the vertical in order to increase resistance to artillery fire. It began at the middle deck (1.52 m above the waterline) and terminated at the lower deck level (0.69 m below the water lines at standard draught). Its armour plates had a thickness of 356 mm abreast the main armament magazines, reducing to 330 mm abreast the machinery spaces.

The transverse armoured bulkhead located forward of 'A' turret had a thickness of 305 mm, while the bulkhead at the aft end of the citadel was 254 mm thick. At the middle deck level over the magazines, 159 mm thick armour plates were laid, while the engine rooms were protected by horizontal armour 95.2 mm thick. The steering gear compartment was protected by 101.6 mm armour plates, while the lower funnel uptakes were covered by 203 mm thick armour.

The barbettes of the main armament turrets had a thickness ranging from 330 mm to 381 mm. Turret faces were covered with 406.4 mm thick plates, the sides with 279.4 mm armour, the rear walls with 228.6 mm plates, while turret roofs were protected by 158.7 mm thick plates.

The secondary armament turrets were not as well protected, with their armour thickness ranging from 25 mm to 38.1 mm.

The front section of the conning tower was covered with 305 mm thick armour, the sides were 356 mm thick and the rear section was protected by 254 mm armour. Its armoured roof was 165.1 mm thick, while the communication tube connecting it with the fire control position was covered by 152.4 mm armour.

The anti-torpedo belt (effectively an internal anti-torpedo bulge), consisted of an outer air space and an inner buoyancy space, providing additional protection, covering the space between the hull plating and the 38 mm thick longitudinal torpedo bulkhead, to the bottom of the hull. It extended upwards to the middle deck with the main armoured belt and its structural supports.

Nelson in a bow port side view. The main battery turrets are clearly visible.

Machinery

The placement of main armament turrets forward required the machinery to be located in the aft section of the hull. As a result, the designers once again decided to adopt a rather unusual solution – in this case, placing the engine rooms forward of the two boiler rooms. This allowed for the turbines and their reduction gearing to be installed in the beamier section of the hull and place the funnel well towards the stern, to prevent the smoke from interfering with the bridge structure. The disadvantage of such a layout was the necessity of using considerably longer and thus heavier drive shafts.

Each of the ships had two boiler rooms, which were longitudinally divided into two compartments, with two Admiralty three-drum oil-fired boilers in each of them. They supplied steam at a working pressure of 17.6 kG/cm² (250 PSI) and temperature of 150° C (302° F), powering two Brown-Curtis steam turbine units with a total power output of 46,000 SHP. The turbines and their reduction gear units were in four compartments, separated by transverse bulkheads and a centreline bulkhead, which also divided the boiler rooms. The geared turbines drove two shafts, each with a three-bladed propeller. The maximum attained speed was 23 knots.

Electric power for all shipboard purposes was provided by four 300 kW generators, each generating 220 V DC, driven by steam turbines located in separate compartments of the boiler and engine rooms. Additionally, there were two diesel-powered generators located in the compartments between 'B' and 'X' turrets.

Trials of battleship *Rodney* in 1927 (standard displacement)

Date	Power output (SHP)	RPM	Speed (kn)	Displacement (tons)
30.08.1927	18,274	123.10	18.59	33,785
30.08.1927	14,931	114.40	17.44	33,775
30.08.1927	9,982	97.94	14.99	33,717
30.08.1927	6,590	87.70	13.30	33,765
01.09.1927	28,030	140.10	21.02	33,660
02.09.1927	36,766	153.44	22.66	33,430
07.09.1927	45,614	163.00	23.80	33,660

Trials of battleship *Nelson* in 1927 (standard displacement)

Date	Power output (SHP)	RPM	Speed (kn)	Displacement (tons)
21.05.1927	6,296	83.35	12.60	33,859
21.05.1927	9,218	94.96	14.41	33,870
21.05.1927	14,605	110.90	16.83	33,884
21.05.1927	18,662	121.19	18.30	33,913
23.05.1927	27,492	136.97	20.44	33,873
24.05.1927	36,920	150.67	22.40	33,624
26.05.1927	46,031	161.60	23.55	33,636

Main armament

The concentration of all main armament guns in triple turrets, all mounted forward of the bridge structure, allowed for a larger number of guns to be carried on a relatively small hull. Weight savings, achieved mainly by shortening the armoured citadel, were of paramount importance when the ship was designed to such strictly imposed limits. The disadvantage of such a solution was the enormous forces affecting that section of the hull when salvos were being fired. Blast from the guns was also a significant problem. This was most noticeable when the turrets were trained abaft the beam and fired, inflicting damage on the superstructure and the deck fittings.

The turrets themselves were built by the Vickers Group. These were a novel design with significant improvements over the previous ones used by the Royal Navy. They were better armoured and more importantly had modern systems that prevented uncontrolled cordite ignition. Their design allowed for a maximum elevation of +40°, which ensured a range of more than 36,000 m. Each turret was fitted with a 41-foot optical rangefinder, which allowed for independent fire under extreme circumstances. The total weight of a single turret ranged from 1,487 tons to 1,507 tons depending on its position.

The 406 mm (16 in) 'BL 16"/45 Mark I' guns were made by Sir W. G. Armstrong Whitworth & Company at Elswick, Vickers at Barrow-in-Furness, William Beardmore & Company at Dalmuir and the Royal Gun Factory at Woolwich. Total weight of the gun was 109.7 tons and its overall length was 18,852 mm. Their range was up to 36,375 m at a muzzle velocity of 797 m/s and an elevation of +40°. It is interesting to note, that these were the last wire-wound British naval guns.

The shell rooms had a capacity of 100 rounds per barrel. The barrel life was estimated at 250 rounds. Interestingly, both ships were commissioned guns with Mk I rifling, which were gradually exchanged for the examples with Mk II rifling (not to be confused with the BL 16"/45 Mark II, a different gun) with different chamber volume and grooving. This resulted in both types being used simultaneously on board the ships. *Rodney* was the first to receive Mk II-rifled guns in 1937. Two guns were replaced in 'B' turret, meaning there were two Mk II-rifled guns and one Mk I mounted in the same turret for a period. The guns were replaced again in 1942, when new Mk II ones were mounted in 'A' turret.

Nelson underwent similar modifications. First, in 1944, the guns were replaced in 'B' and 'X' turrets, and then, in 1945, 'A' turret.

Nelson photographed in the mid-1930s. The letters NE painted on the roof of the X turret are visible.

Main armament turret data

Revolving weight	1,487-1,507 t
Revolving path diameter	10.06 m
Barbette diameter	11.43 m
Distance apart gun axes	2,489 m
Recoil distance	1.13 m
Elevation speed	10°/s

406 mm gun data

Bore	406.4 mm
Length OA	18,852 mm
Barrel length	18,288 mm
Length chamber	3,187.7 mm
Volume chamber	576.9 dm³
Weight	109.733 kg
Grooves	3.43 mm x 9,576 mm
Projectile weight	929 kg
Propellant charge	224.5 kg
Muzzle velocity	797 m/s
Working pressure	3150 kg/cm²
Barrel life	250 rounds
Range	36,375 m
Elevation	-3° to +40°

Secondary armament

The secondary armament of the battleships *Nelson* and *Rodney* consisted of twelve 152 mm Mk XXII BL guns mounted in six twin Mk XVIII turrets.

Considering the fact that the secondary armament of the Royal Navy capital ships was hitherto mounted in hull casemates, it was a relatively innovative solution, providing wider arcs of fire and much better protection of the gun crews against splinters.

Particularly important was the ability to elevate the barrels at high angles, up to +60°, which in effect made the guns dual-purpose weapons allowing them to lay an anti-aircraft barrage as well as defend against surface vessels. The turrets were mounted three on each side abreast of the funnel and mainmast. Their magazines were behind the boiler rooms directly under the turrets themselves which allowed for expeditious hoisting of ammunition (150 rounds per barrel). A significant drawback of these thoroughly modern turrets, however, was their weak armour. This gave rise to concerns that even in the case of a single hit, their close concentration may have led to the entire battery on one side being put out of action. In practice this never happened, but it remained a serious threat.

A single gun weighed 9,157 kg and had an overall length of 7,867.1 mm. At the muzzle velocity of 902 m/s, its range was 23,590 m.

Secondary armament Mk XVIII turret data

Revolving weight	86,000 kg
Revolving path diameter	4.27 m
Barbette diameter	5.41 m
Distance apart gun axes	1.98 m
Recoil distance	0.42 m
Elevation speed	8°/s

152 mm Mk XXII BL gun data

Bore	152.4 mm
Length OA	7,867 mm
Barrel length	7,620 mm
Length chamber	1,036 mm
Volume chamber	28.7 dm³
Weight	9,157 kg
Grooves	1.17 mm x 9,548 mm
Projectile weight	45.36 kg
Propellant charge	14.06 kg
Muzzle velocity	902 m/s
Working pressure	3,230 kg/cm²
Barrel life	700 rounds
Range	23,590 n (+45°)
Elevation	+60°

Anti-aircraft armament

In the initial period of their service, the anti-aircraft armament of the *Nelson* class battleships consisted of six 120 mm (4.7 in) Mk VIII guns. Two were mounted on the quarterdeck and four on the shelter deck of the superstructure. The allowance was 175 rounds per barrel, as well as 150 star and 20 smoke shells per ship. These guns, on single Mk XII mountings, were only carried as the armament of the battleships considered here and the minelaying cruiser *Adventure*, and remained on board throughout the entire period of their service. One of their most important upgrades was fitting of splinter shields during the war.

The heavy anti-aircraft armament was complemented by eight single 40 mm pom-pom mountings, four of which were on platforms on the bridge structure and four on the rear part of the shelter deck. With time, the anti-aircraft armament of both ships changed considerably. The first significant modification was during the re-armament in 1933–1934, when two eight-barrelled Mk V 40 mm pom-pom gun mounts were fitted abreast the funnel. Another was introduced a year later, when two 12.7 mm (0.5 in) Vickers multiple machine gun mountings were fitted on the after corners of the bridge structure. In 1939, a third eight-barrelled Mk V 40 mm pom-pom mounting was fitted on *Nelson*'s quarterdeck. In addition, two Mk VI eight-barrel 40 mm pom-pom mountings were fitted in place of the aft secondary armament director control towers. At the same time, four Mk I 178 mm UP (Unrotated Projectile) launchers were fitted on the roofs of the main armament 'B' and 'X' turrets.

Further modifications of the armament were introduced at the turn of 1941 and 1942. The UP projectors, which had turned to be a failure, were removed. In their place, a sixth Mk VI 40 mm pom-pom mounting was fitted on the roof of 'B' turret. In addition, the anti-aircraft armament was strengthened by thirteen 20 mm Oerlikon guns.

Further modifications of *Nelson*'s anti-aircraft armament took place in September 1943. Two 12.7 mm machine gun mountings were removed. Instead, 26 more 20 mm Oerlikon mountings were fitted in almost every corner of the ship.

The final modification of *Nelson*'s anti-aircraft armament took place at the turn of 1944 and 1945 when the ship was in the USA. Then, apart from significant modifications of the ship's equipment, twenty-four 20 mm Oerlikon mountings were fitted. Moreover, four four-barrelled Mk NI Bofors 40 mm mountings were fitted abreast the bridge structure and funnel.

Similar modifications were made to her sister ship *Rodney*.

In 1940, apart from her standard anti-aircraft armament, the battleship was fitted with another eight-barrelled 40 mm pom-pom mounting, and two single 20 mm cannon fitted on the roof of 'B' turret.

More significant modernisation of the armament took place in September 1941, when the aforementioned 20 mm guns were removed from the roof of 'B' turret and replaced by a four-barrelled Mk VII 40 mm pom-pom. At the same time, similarly to *Nelson*, she had two Mk VI 40 mm pom-pom mountings fitted in the place of the aft secondary armament director control towers. In the first half of 1942, seventeen 20 mm Oerlikon guns were fitted and the ineffective 12.7 mm machine gun mountings were removed. The following year, four 20 mm gun mountings were fitted, and in August another 35 single 20 mm Oerlikons and 5 twin Mk V mountings of the same calibre were added. The final modification took place in 1944, when two more 20 mm Oerlikons were fitted.

General characteristics of the anti-aircraft armament discussed above are presented in the tables below:

Stern shot of the Nelson. The structure of the mainmast, as it looked during the initial period of the ship's service, is clearly visible. The letters of the ship's name on the starboard side are also worthy of attention.

40 mm Mk VI pom-pom gun data

Bore	40 mm
Barrel length	1.57 m
Weight of Mk VI mount	11.19 t
Projectile weight	1.30 kg
Propellant charge	0.13 kg
Muzzle velocity	732 m/s
Barrel life	7,200 rounds
Horizontal range	4,572 m
Vertical range	3,960 m

Elevation	-10° to +80°
Rate of fire	96-98 rounds/m

40 mm Mk NI (US) Bofors gun data

Bore	40 mm
Barrel length	3.96 m
Weight	11,324 to 11,596 kg
Projectile weight	0.91 kg
Propellant charge	0.25 kg
Muzzle velocity	881 m/s
Barrel life	9500 rounds
Horizontal range	11,425 m
Vertical range	6,800 m
Elevation	-15° to +90°
Rate of fire	150 rounds/m

20 mm Mk II Oerlikon gun data

Bore	20 mm
Barrel length	1.45 m
Weight	0.78 tons
Projectile weight	0.12 kg
Propellant charge	0.027 kg
Muzzle velocity	830 m/s
Barrel life	9,000 rounds
Range horizontal +35°	4,387 m
Range vertical +70°	3,048 m
Elevation	-5° to +87°
Rate of fire	450 rounds/m

20 mm Mk V Oerlikon gun data

Bore	20 mm
Barrel length	1.45 m
Weight	1,200 kg
Projectile weight	0.12 kg
Propellant charge	0.027 kg
Muzzle velocity	830 m/s
Barrel life	9,000 rounds

Range horizontal	4,387 m
Range vertical	3,048 m
Elevation	-10 +70 degrees
Rate of fire	450 rounds/m

Mk I UP (Unrotated Projectile) projector data

Diameter	178 mm
Number of launching tubes	20
Rocket length	81.3 cm
Rocket weight	15.9 kg
Range	900 m
Sink rate	5-7 m/s
Explosive charge	0.24 kg
Weight of mounting	4 tons

Both battleship also had four 47 mm Hotchkiss saluting guns mounted on the deck aft of the bridge superstructure. They had no combat value and were only used when the ships performed representative duties. They were removed during the war.

Rodney *firing her 152 mm and 120 mm guns in 1939. The ship had already undergone another modification of the anti-aircraft armament, receiving another 40 mm pom-pom mount installed on the quarterdeck.*

A starboard shot of Rodney *in the summer of 1940. The ship had already undergone a partial modification of the anti-aircraft armament. She was armed with three eight-barreled 40 mm pom-pom mounts on the sides of the funnel and on the quarterdeck, two 20 mm guns on the roof of 'B' turret, and two four-barreled 12.7 mm gun mounts on the sides of the conning tower.*

A port side shot of Rodney *in 1942.*

Torpedo Armament

Nelson class battleships were also armed with torpedoes. There were two underwater Mk I launchers with an unusual diameter of 622.3 mm, fitted below deck in the bow section. Each battleship carried 12 torpedoes, each with a warhead containing 337 kg of TNT.

Fire Control System

Each battleship had two main armament director control towers, each with a 15-foot rangefinder. One was on the bridge and the other at the after end of the superstructure. Two similar secondary armament director control towers, each with a 12-foot rangefinder, were located at the top of the bridge and another two at the aft end of superstructure. An alternative main battery fire control position was in an armoured hood on the conning tower.

Anti-aircraft armament fire control positions were located in two small towers positioned on both sides of the director control tower platform of the bridge superstructure.

In the initial period of the ships' service, a 12-foot high-angle rangefinder was fitted on the upper platform. Fire control equipment was also complemented by 41-foot rangefinder in each of the main armament turrets and two 9-foot tactical rangefinders on the forward director control tower platform. For control of the torpedo armament there were two towers with 15-foot rangefinders positioned abreast of the funnel.

Radar Equipment

During their service the battleships *Rodney* and *Nelson* were fitted with various types of radar. This included a long-range Type 79Y early air warning radar, with a wavelength of 7 m and two separate transmitting

Rodney *during a cruise on the Firth of Forth in August 1940.*

and receiving antennas, consisting of two parallel dipoles with reflectors. The receiver had an A-scope display. It was fitted to the battleship *Rodney* in 1938, and it is worthy of mention that she was the first battleship of the Royal Navy to be fitted with such equipment. A later modification of Type 79Y was Type 279 radar. Like its predecessor, this early air warning radar used a wavelength of 7 m – the main difference was the addition of a GL1 radar rangefinder to improve accuracy of the anti-aircraft gunlaying. It was fitted to the battleship *Rodney* and replaced the 79Y radar.

Another radar that was part of the ship's equipment was the Type 281, which was also used to detect aerial targets. It used a wavelength of 3.5 m, and its distinctive rectangular truss antennas (one transmitting and the other receiving) were mounted on mastheads. This radar, fitted to both *Rodney* and *Nelson*, had an A-scope display and GL1 radar rangefinder.

To control anti-aircraft fire both ships had Type 282 radars. These were close-range devices which used a wavelength of 50 cm with two Yagi antennas (one transmitting and one receiving) installed on the roofs of the 40 mm gun directors.

Both battleships were also fitted with Type 283 radar designed to control high-angle anti-aircraft fire. As with the Type 282, the 283 worked on a wavelength of 50 cm and had a double set of Yagi antennas with a reflector, and the receiver was equipped with the ABU (Auto Barrage Unit) indicator.

The Type 284 radar, designed to control low-angle artillery fire, used the same wavelength as the aforementioned Type 283. It also had two sets of antennas (one transmitting and one receiving) made of 24 dipoles with a parabolic reflector installed on the device. It was fitted to both *Rodney* and *Nelson*.

The Type 285 radar, designed to control high-angle anti-aircraft fire, used a wavelength of 50 cm, with six antennas (three transmitting and three receiving ones) and three reflectors installed on the device. It was also fitted to both battleships.

Unique to *Rodney* was the Type 271 surface warning radar, which worked on a wavelength of 10 cm. It had two antennas enclosed in a distinctive perspex "lantern" and an A-scope display.

The final radar unit, fitted to both *Rodney* and *Nelson*, was Type 273 which, like the Type 271 was a surface warning radar, working on a wavelength of 10 cm. It had dual antenna set of parabolic reflectors with a diameter of 1,372 mm, activated by dipoles.

Aircraft facilities

Rodney was equipped with a McTaggart-Scott extending catapult fitted on the roof of 'X' turret, and a 7-ton aircraft handling crane fitted on the port side of the bridge superstructure to lower or hoist seaplanes. The first aircraft to be allocated to *Rodney* was a Fairey IIIF floatplane, followed by a Fairey Swordfish and finally a Supermarine Walrus flying boat. The catapult was removed in 1943.

Nelson was never fitted with any aircraft facilities. However, a crane (different from the one installed on *Rodney*) was fitted on deck on the port side abreast the bridge superstructure.

Service history highlights – HMS *Nelson*

- 28 December, 1922. Keel laid down at Armstrong, Newcastle-on-Tyne.
- 3 September, 1925. Launching ceremony. The battleship was christened by Dame Caroline Bridgeman.
- 21–28 May, 1927. Sea trials at the measured mile in the vicinity of West Looe in Cornwall.
- 30 August, 1927. Another series of sea trials.
- 15 August, 1927. The ship was commissioned into service with the Royal Navy. She began intensive training exercises.
- 21 October, 1927. The battleship became the flagship of Vice-Admiral Hubert Brand, commander of the Royal Navy's Atlantic Fleet. She served in that capacity for fourteen consecutive years, wearing the flags of eight admirals and sailing to many different countries around the world.
- February 1930. *Nelson* took part in the rescue of the Greek ship *Fofo*, carrying a load of coal, which sank on 25 February, 40 nm North-East of Oran.
- 29 March, 1931. Collision with SS *West Wales*.
- March 1932. The battleship became the flagship of the Home Fleet (new name for the Atlantic Fleet).
- 1932 to 1933. The battleship underwent the first major modification, which consisted of alterations to a platform on the forward face of the bridge structure.
- 1933 to 1934. Another modification. The ship was armed with two 40 mm "pom-pom" mountings and new directors, directional rangefinder and a frame antenna were installed.
- January 1934. While leaving Portsmouth, the battleship ran aground on the shoal known as Hamilton Bank (after Lady Hamilton, the lover of Lord Nelson).
- 1934 to 1935. The battleship received two additional 12.7 mm machine gun mountings.
- October 1935. *Nelson* took part in tests of the prototype Walrus amphibious aircraft at Portland and one of these machines landed alongside the battleship.
- May 1937. The battleship took part in the coronation naval review for King George VI at Spithead.
- 1937 to 1938. The ship remained at Portsmouth, where she underwent another refit. Extra armour was fitted, new fire control systems were installed and a ship's crane was installed on the port side.
- February 1938. The battleship, along with her sister ship *Rodney*, paid a visit to Lisbon.
- September 1939. The outbreak of war. The battleship was redeployed to the Shetland Islands area.
- 26 September, 1939. The battleship with the aircraft carrier *Ark Royal* and other ships took part in the rescue of the submarine *Spearfish*. In the North Sea, 150 nm from the coast of Norway, the battleship was attacked by German aircraft.
- 8 October, 1939. The battleship with her sister ship *Rodney* put to sea to take part in an operation to intercept the German battleship *Gneisenau* and the light cruiser *Köln* accompanying her.
- 23–31 October, 1939. The battleship with her sister ship *Rodney* and the battlecruiser *Hood* escorted Norwegian ships. During the operation, on October 30, the battleship was unsuccessfully attacked by the German submarine *U 56*.

- 31 October, 1939. During her stay at Greenock, First Sea Lord, Admiral Sir Dudley Pound and Deputy Chief of the Air Staff, Sir Richard Peirse came on board the battleship to discuss the air and anti-submarine defences of naval bases.
- 23–30 November, 1939. The battleship together with her sister ship *Rodney* and other warships including the battleship *Warspite* and battlecruisers *Repulse* and *Hood* took part in an operation against the German battleships *Scharnhorst* and *Gneisenau*.

- 4 December, 1939. Returning from a patrol in the North Sea, during her approach to Loch Ewe, the battleship activated a magnetic mine. The explosion caused a serious damage.
- January to August 1940. The battleship was repaired and refitted at Portsmouth. Three additional 40 mm pom-pom mountings and four UP launchers were installed.
- September 1940. The battleship left the shipyard and participated in operations off the coast of Norway.
- November 6, 1940. The battleship with her sister ship *Rodney* searched for the German pocket battleship *Admiral Scheer*.
- January to February 1941. The battleships took part in the search for the German battleships *Scharnhorst* and *Gneisenau*.
- 2 March, 1941. The ship, with the battleship *King George V* and light cruisers *Nigeria* and *Dido*, took part in Operation Claymore.
- March 1941. The battleship continued operations against the German battleships *Scharnhorst* and *Gneisenau*.
- 1 April, 1941. *Nelson* was relieved as the Home Fleet flagship by the battleship *King George V*. Soon thereafter she departed to provide cover for a convoy heading around Africa for the Far East.
- June 1941. The ship rejoined the Home Fleet.
- July 1941. *Nelson* was transferred to Force H and redeployed to Gibraltar, where she took part in Operation Substance (providing cover for a relief convoy heading for besieged Malta).
- 8 August, 1941. The battleship relieved the battlecruiser *Renown* as the flagship of Force H.
- 24–30 September, 1941. The battleship took part in Operation Halberd, escorting a convoy heading for besieged Malta. During the convoy, on September 27, the battleship was hit by a torpedo launched by an Italian aircraft, and heavily damaged.
- 30 September, 1941. The damaged *Nelson*, escorted by other ships, returned to Gibraltar. Her draught forward was 40 feet.
- 2 October, 1941. The battleship was docked for temporary repairs which allowed her safe return to Great Britain. On the previous day she was relieved as a flagship by the battleship *Rodney*.
- 23 November, 1941. The ship arrived at Rosyth, where she was repaired and refitted at the local shipyard. Her anti-aircraft armament was strengthened and radar equipment was installed.
- 22 April, 1942. Following repairs the ship went to Scapa Flow to rejoin the Home Fleet. Soon thereafter the battleship was transferred to the Eastern Fleet.
- 31 May, 1942. The battleship left the Clyde to escort a convoy heading for Freetown. Later, it was planned that she was to sail around Africa.
- June 1942. The battleship escorted a convoy heading for Freetown. Upon arrival she was ordered to abort the mission and return to home waters.
- 26 July, 1942. *Nelson* returned to Scapa Flow and soon thereafter departed to escort another convoy heading for Malta.
- 9–15 August, 1942. The battleship took part in Operation Pedestal (delivery of supplies to Malta).
- October 1942. *Nelson* was assigned to take part in Operation Torch, the landing of Allied troops in North Africa.
- 8–16 November, 1942. The ship took part in Operation Torch, serving as the flagship of Force H for a period. On 15 November she became the flagship of Force H and served in that role until May 1943.
- November to December, 1942. The battleship provided cover for shipping between Gibraltar and Mers el Kebir.
- January to May 1943. *Nelson* operated in the Mediterranean.
- 10 July, 1943. The battleship took part in Operation Husky, the Allied invasion of Sicily.

- 31 August, 1943. Along with her sister ship *Rodney*, she bombarded the region of Reggio di Calabria on the Italian mainland.
- September 1943. The battleship took an active part in operations against Italy.
- 9 September, 1943. *Nelson* covered the Allied landing at Salerno.
- 29 September, 1943. Italian unconditional surrender was signed on board the battleship.
- October 1943. The ship returned to home waters, where she underwent maintenance.
- January to May 1944. The ship remained in home waters, being stationed at Scapa Flow, Clyde and Rosyth.
- June 1944. The battleship was assigned to support the Allied landing force near the coast of Normandy.
- 11–18 June, 1944. The battleship bombarded German positions.
- 18 June, 1944. During her passage to Portsmouth the battleship detonated two acoustic mines. Their explosions caused substantial damage.
- 22 June, 1944. The battleship was dispatched to the USA for a major refit.
- August 1944 to January 1945. The ship remained at Philadelphia Naval Yard, where she was refitted and her armament strengthened. Additional 20 mm anti-aircraft guns and four 40 mm Bofors mountings were installed.
- January to March 1945. The battleship underwent a refit at Portsmouth.
- April 1945. She was assigned to join the East Indies Fleet and take part in operations against the Japanese forces.
- April 29, 1945. The battleship left Portsmouth and headed to the Far East via Gibraltar, Malta (where she commenced a programme of working up in preparation for action against the Japanese), Alexandria, Port Said and the Suez Canal to Colombo, where she arrived on 9 July.
- 12 July, 1945. She became the flagship of the East Indies Fleet.
- 24–26 July, 1945. She took part in the bombardment of Phuket Island near the Malaya Peninsula.
- 2 September, 1945. During her stay at Penang, a Japanese delegation arrived on board to negotiate the surrender of Japanese forces in Singapore.
- 12 September, 1945. The formal document surrendering the Japanese forces in South-East Asia was signed on board the battleship.
- 20 September, 1945. She was relieved as the flagship by the battleship *Howe* and left for home.
- 13 October, 1945. The battleship arrived at Scapa Flow.
- 17 November, 1945. The ship was redeployed to Plymouth.
- 27 December, 1945. *Nelson* moved to Portland.
- 14 August, 1946. She became the flagship of the Home Fleet Training Squadron.
- 20 October, 1946. The battleship was reduced to reserve.
- 19 May, 1948. She was used as bombing target for heavy armour-piercing bombs.
- 5 January, 1949. The ship was sold for scrap.
- 15 March, 1949. The battleship arrived at Inverkeithing where she was to be scrapped.
- December 1949. The partially dismantled wreck was towed to Troon, where the scrapping was concluded.

Battle Honours: *Nelson*
- MALTA CONVOYS 1941–42
- NORTH AFRICA 1942–43
- MEDITERRANEAN 1943
- SICILY 1943
- SALERNO 1943
- NORMANDY 1944
Motto: *Palmam Qui Meruit Ferat*: "Let him bear the palm who deserves it".

Service history highlights – HMS *Rodney*

- 28 December, 1922. The keel was laid down at Cammell Laird shipyard at Birkenhead.
- 17 December, 1925. Launching ceremony. The battleship was christened by Princess Mary, Viscountess Lascelles.
- 21–26 May, 1927. Sea trials from the Walker shipyard on the Tyne.
- 9 August, 1927. Completion of sea trials.
- 14 September, 1927. The battleship returned to the Birkenhead shipyard.
- 7 December, 1927. The ship was commissioned into service with the Royal Navy and assigned to the 2nd Battle Squadron of the Atlantic Fleet.
- 4 May, 1930. The battleship became temporary flagship of the Atlantic Fleet.
- June 1930. She was assigned to escort the British Parliamentary Delegation to Iceland for the 1000th Anniversary Celebrations of the Icelandic Parliament.
- July 1931. *Rodney* again replaced her sister ship *Nelson* as the flagship, after the latter had collided with steamer *West Wales*.
- 1931 to 1932. The battleship underwent a modernisation. Rangefinders were installed on the bridge platform. A wireless set was replaced by a more modern one and high-angle control positions were also fitted.

- 1932 to 1933. Another modernisation. A new compass platform was built over the admiral's bridge.
- 1933 to 1934. The ship received two eight-barrelled 40 mm pom-pom mountings fitted abreast the funnel.
- October 1934. She again replaced her sister ship *Nelson* as flagship.
- 1934 to 1935. While at the shipyard the ship received two 12.7 heavy machine gun mountings.
- February 1938. The battleship, along with her sister ship *Nelson*, paid a visit to Lisbon. In the same year, during an overhaul, aircraft facilities were fitted.
- September 1939. Outbreak of war. The battleship was redeployed to the Shetland Islands area.
- October 8, 1939. The battleship with her sister ship *Nelson* put to sea to take part in the operation to intercept the German battleship *Gneisenau* and the light cruiser *Köln*.
- 23–31 October, 1939. The battleship with her sister ship *Nelson* and the battlecruiser *Hood* escorted Norwegian ships.
- 23–30 November, 1939. The battleship together with her sister ship *Nelson* and other warships including the battleship *Warspite* and battlecruisers *Repulse* and *Hood* took part in the operation against the German battleships *Scharnhorst* and *Gneisenau*. During the operation *Rodney* developed serious rudder defects.
- December 1939. The battleship underwent repairs in a shipyard.
- 1 January, 1940. Following the refit, she rejoined the fleet and assumed the role of the flagship, while *Nelson* was repaired.
- April 1940. The battleship began operations in Norwegian waters due to fears of a German invasion.
- 9 April, 1940. *Rodney* was hit aft by a bomb off Bergen. It penetrated the weather, the upper and finally the armoured deck forward of the funnel and exploded causing damage and starting a fire.
- April to June 1940. The battleship continued her operations in Norwegian Waters.
- 6 November, 1940. Along with her sister ship *Rodney*, the battleship took part in the search for the German pocket battleship *Admiral Scheer*.

- January 1941. *Rodney* underwent an overhaul.
- January to March 1941. The battleship took part in operations against the German battleships *Scharnhorst* and *Gneisenau*.
- 24 May, 1941. She took part in the search for the German battleship *Bismarck*, which, along with the heavy cruiser *Prinz Eugen*, was making her way into the North Atlantic. During the pursuit *Rodney* joined the battleship *King George V*.
- 27 May, 1941. Along with the battleship *King George V* and other vessels, *Rodney* sank the *Bismarck*.
- 29 May, 1941. The battleship arrived at Greenock with slight damage sustained during the battle and fuel tanks almost empty.
- 3 June, 1941. The battleship, accompanied by the *Windsor Castle*, headed for Halifax, where she arrived on 11 June.
- 12 June, 1941. The ship arrived at Boston Navy Yard, where she was refitted. Her armament was also modernised.
- 12 August, 1941. The refit was concluded and the ship underwent trials.
- 24 August, 1941. She arrived at Bermuda, where she worked-up and underwent a series of trials.
- 24 September, 1941. The ship arrived at Gibraltar where she joined Force H.
- 24–30 September, 1941. She, along with the battleships *Nelson* and *Prince of Wales*, took part in Operation Halberd, the objective of which was to provide cover to a convoy heading to the besieged Malta.

An excellent photograph showing the main battery turrets of the battleship Rodney. *Details of the seaplane catapult installed on the roof of 'X' turret and the 20 mm anti-aircraft gun mounts on the roof of 'B' turret are clearly visible. Her sister ship* Nelson *can be seen in the background.*

- 1 October, 1941. Replaced *Nelson* as a flagship, after the latter was damaged by aerial torpedo in the aforementioned operation.
- 16 October, 1941. The battleship left Gibraltar taking part in Operation Callboy (delivery of torpedo bomber aircraft to Malta).
- November 1941. The ship ceased to be Force H flagship and returned to home waters.
- November 1941. The battleship began operations against German forces in the far North.
- February to May 1942. She was refitted in Liverpool. Her anti-aircraft armament was strengthened and new radar equipment was installed.
- May 1942. Following the completion of the refit, the ship headed to Scapa Flow and rejoined the Home Fleet. Shortly thereafter, as with sister ship *Nelson*, *Rodney* was assigned to the Eastern Fleet.
- June 1942. *Rodney* escorted a convoy heading to Freetown. Upon arrival at her destination orders were received to abort and return to home waters.
- June to July 1942. While she was in the shipyard her anti-aircraft armament was further strengthened.
- 16 July, 1942. The battleship returned to Scapa Flow and shortly thereafter departed to provide cover for a convoy heading to Malta.
- 9–15 August, 1942. The ship took part in Operation Pedestal (carrying supplies to the besieged Malta).
- October 1942. The battleship was assigned to take part in Operation Torch (Allied landing in North Africa).
- 8–16 November, 1942. The ship took part in Operation Torch, shelling, among other targets, batteries at Oran.
- November to December 1942. The battleship operated in the Mediterranean.
- May 1943. She rejoined the Home Fleet.
- June 1943. The ship again operated with Force H.
- 23 June, 1943. *Rodney* arrived at Gibraltar.
- 10 July, 1943. The battleship took part in Operation Husky (Allied landing in Sicily).

Starboard side view of Nelson.

- August 1943. She underwent a short overhaul and her anti-aircraft armament was strengthened.
- 31 August, 1943. Along with her sister ship *Nelson*, she bombarded enemy defences at Reggio.
- September 1943. She took active part in operations against Italy, in support of the Allied landing at Salerno.
- October 1943. The battleship returned to home waters and rejoined the Home Fleet.
- June 1944. She was incorporated into the invasion force in Normandy, bombarding Benerville and Houlgate batteries on D-Day.
- 2 July, 1944. She bombarded enemy troop concentrations.
- 8 July, 1944. The battleship bombarded enemy defences at Caen.
- 12 August, 1944. She bombarded German shore batteries on Alderney.
- September 1944. The battleship became the flagship of the Home Fleet and was assigned to the covering force for supply convoys to the Soviet Union.
- April 1945. Reduced to reserve due to machinery problems.
- August 1946. Disarmed while in reserve.
- March 1947. Sold for scrap.
- 26 March, 1948. Arrived at Inverkeithing for scrapping.

Battle Honours: *Rodney*
- QUEBEC 1759
- SYRIA 1840
- CRIMEA 1854
- NORWAY 1940
- ATLANTIC 1940–41
- BISMARCK ACTION 1941
- MALTA CONVOYS 1941–42
- NORTH AFRICA 1942–43
- SICILY 1943
- SALERNO 1943
- MEDITERRANEAN 1943
- NORMANDY 1944
- ENGLISH CHANNEL 1944
- ARCTIC 1944
  Motto: *Non Genarant Aquilae Columbas*: "Eagles do not breed doves"

General characteristics of the battleships *Nelson* and *Rodney* (in 1927)

	Nelson	*Rodney*
Shipyard	Armstrong, Newcastle-on-Tyne	Cammell Laird, Birkenhead
Laid down	28.12.1922	28.12.1922
Launched	03.09.1925	17.12.1925
Commissioned	15.08.1927	07.12.1927
Designed displacement	32.800 t	32.800 t
Standard displacement	33,313 t	33,370 t
Full load	38,400 t	38,316 t
Length OA	216.55 m	216.61 m
Length BP	201.3 m	201.3 m
Beam	32.33 m	32.33 m
Mean draught	8.56 m	8.56 m
Propulsion	2 Brown-Curtis geared steam turbine sets, 8 Admiralty 3-drum oil-fired boilers, 2 shafts	2 Brown-Curtis geared steam turbine sets, 8 Admiralty 3-drum oil-fired boilers, 2 shafts
Power output	46,671 shp	46,248 shp
Bunker capacity	3,900 t	3,900 t
Endurance at 12 kn	14,300 nmi	14,300 nmi
Endurance at 16 kn	7,000 nmi	7,000 nmi
Endurance at 20 kn	5,500 nmi	5,500 nmi
Maximum speed	23.55 kn	23.80 kn

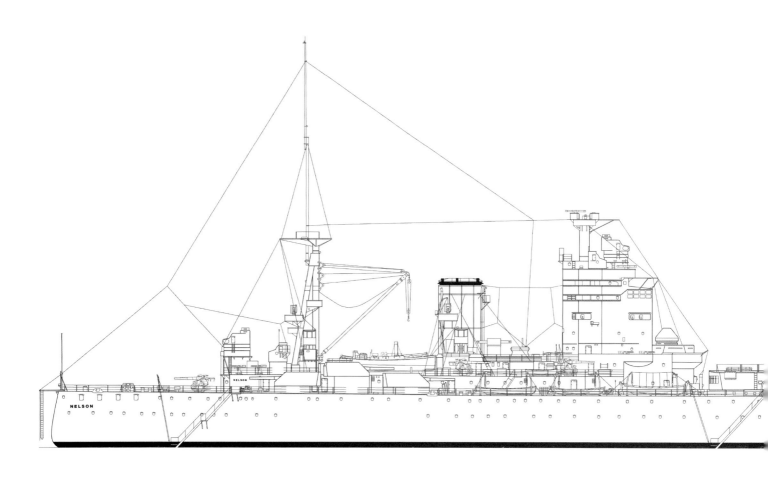

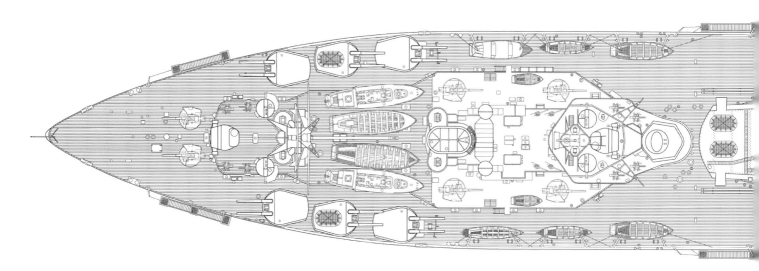

General arrangements HMS *Nelson* 1927.

1/550 scale

Starboard side view

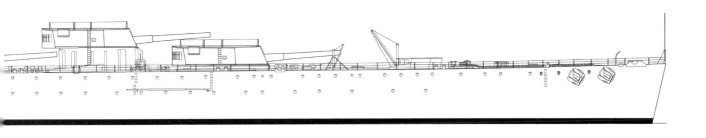

Top view

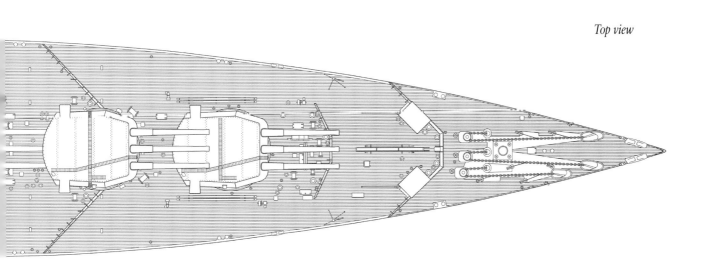

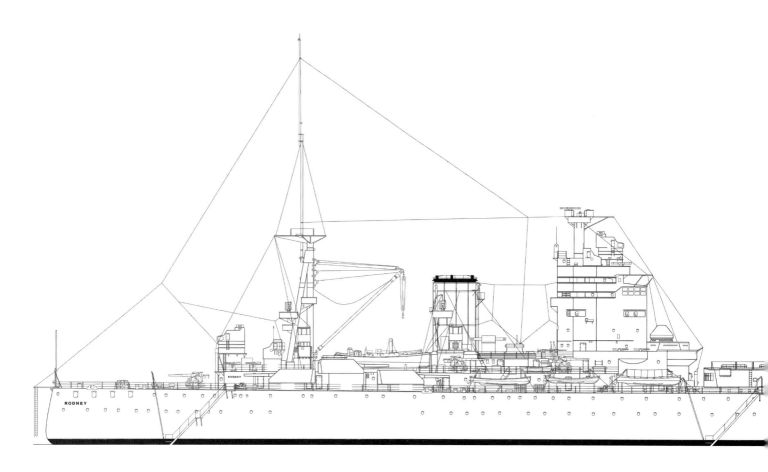

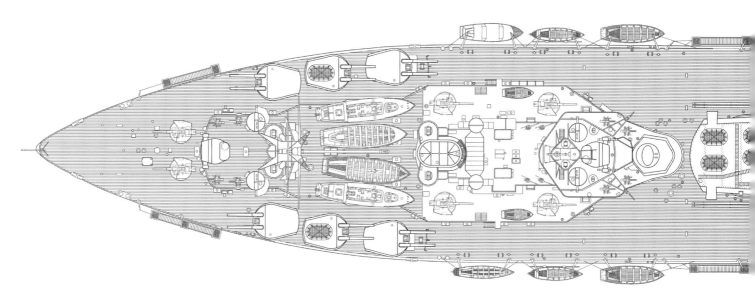

General arrangements HMS *Rodney* 1928.

1/550 scale

Starboard side view

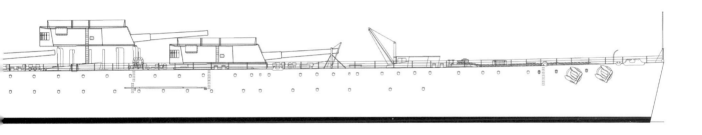

Top view

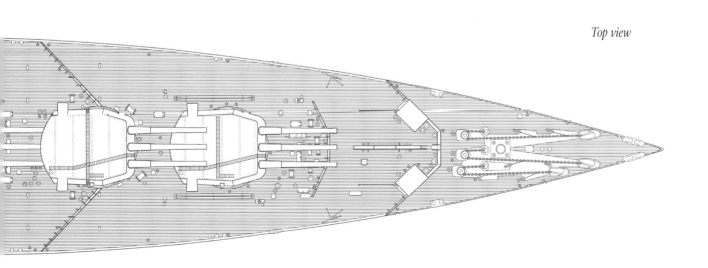

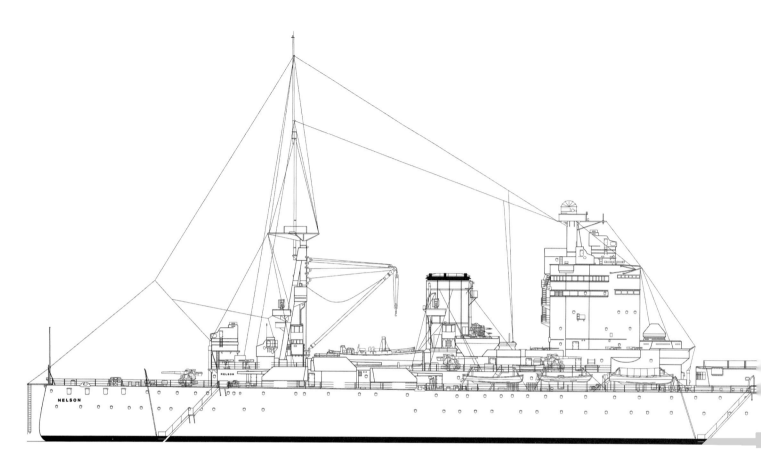

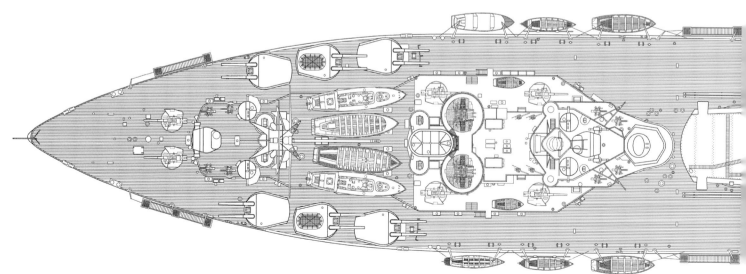

General arrangements HMS *Nelson* 1934.

1/550 scale

Starboard side view

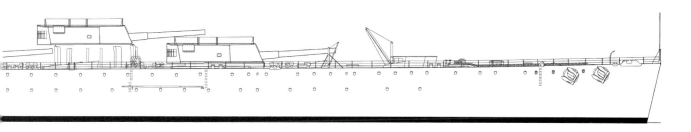

Top view

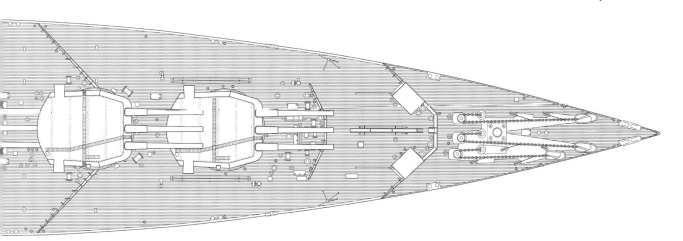

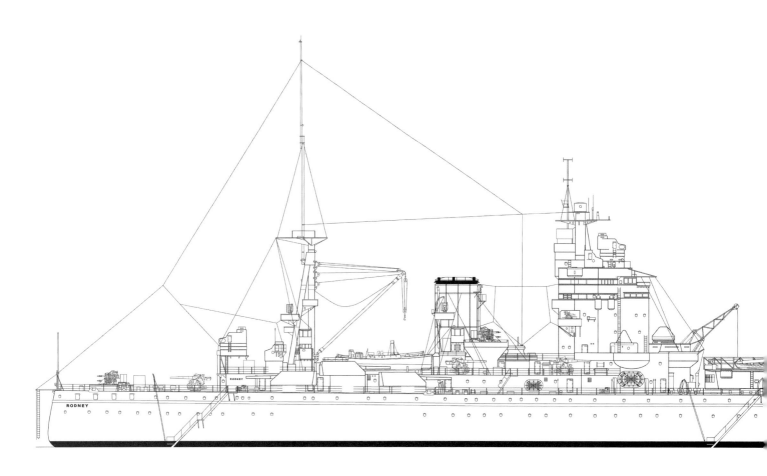

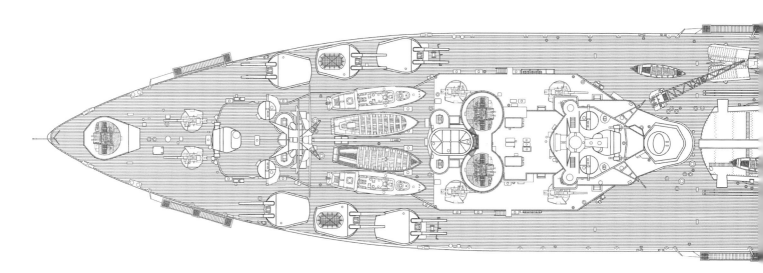

General arrangements HMS *Rodney* 1940.

1/550 scale

Starboard side view

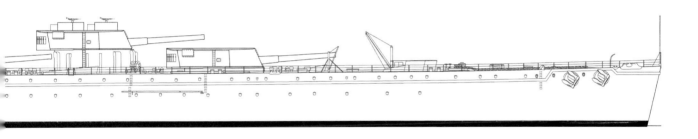

Top view

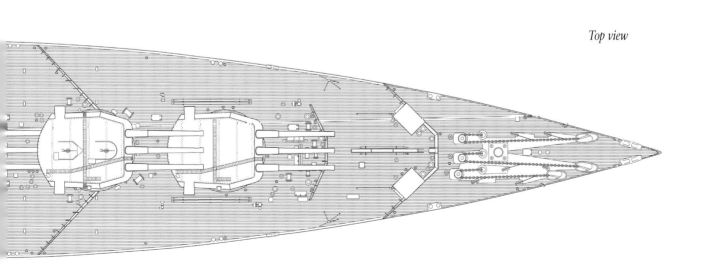

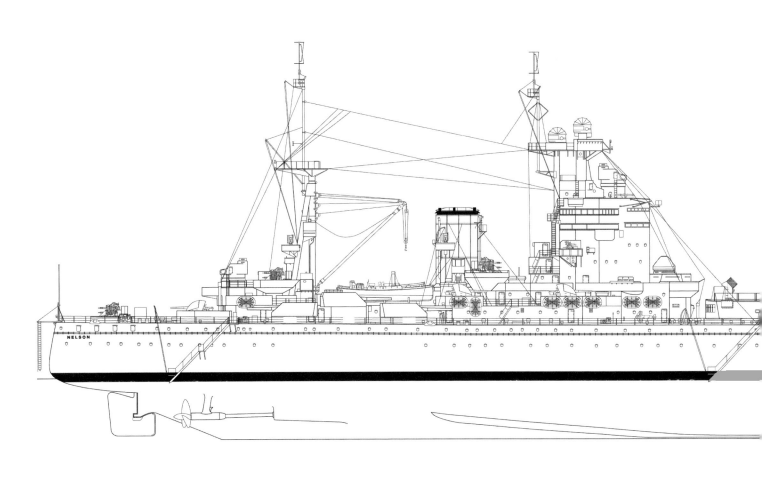

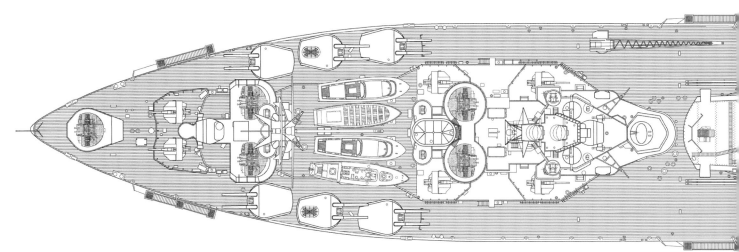

General arrangements HMS *Nelson* 1940.

1/550 scale

Starboard side view

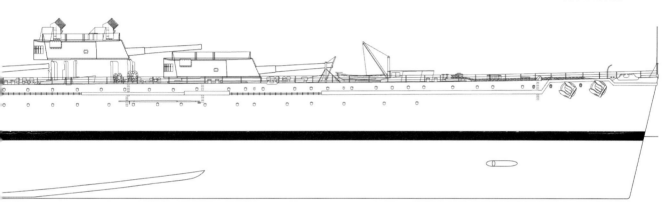

Top view

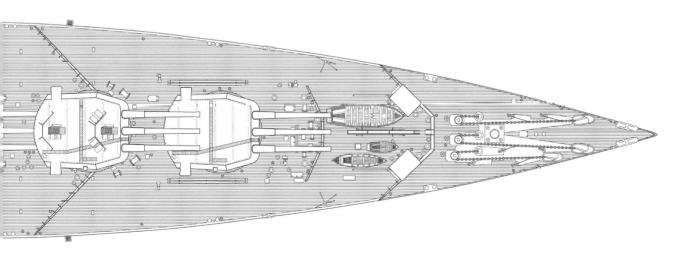

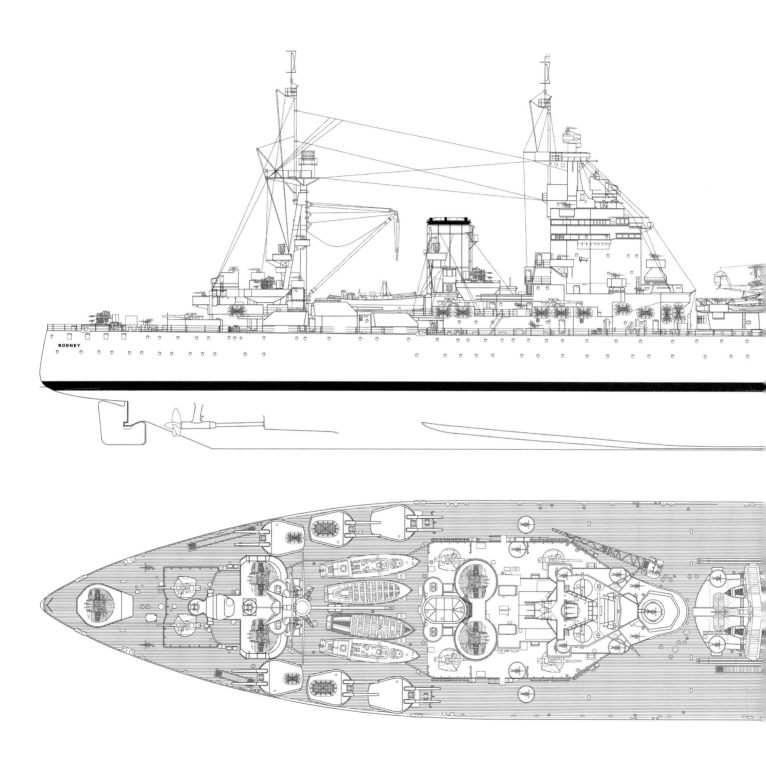

RODNEY

General arrangements HMS *Rodney* 1942.

1/550 scale

Starboard side view

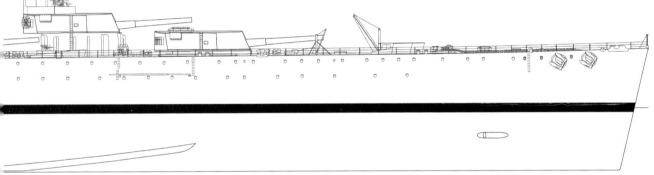

Top view

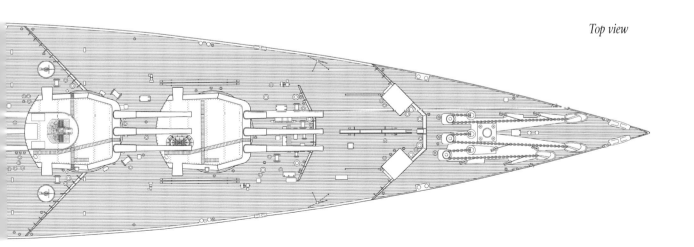

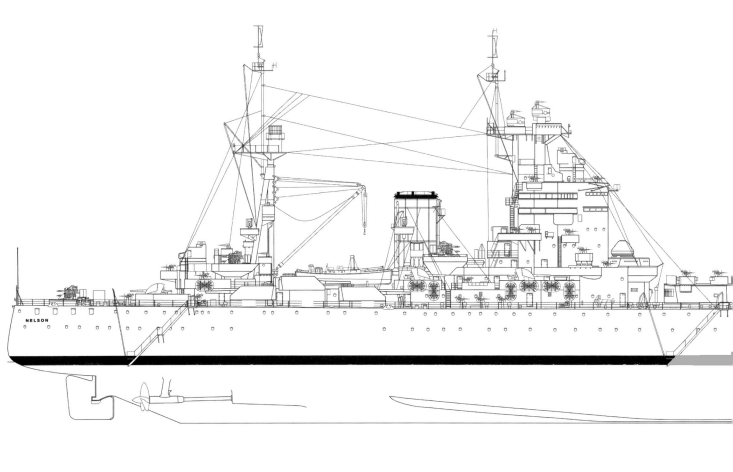
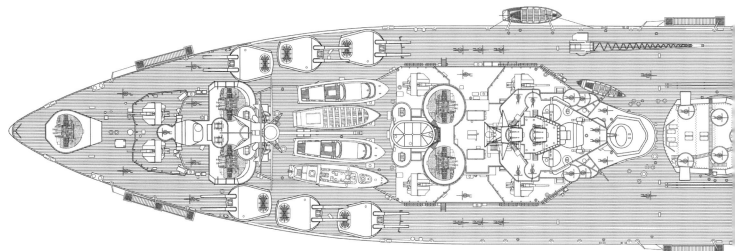

General arrangements HMS *Nelson* 1943.

1/550 scale

Starboard side view

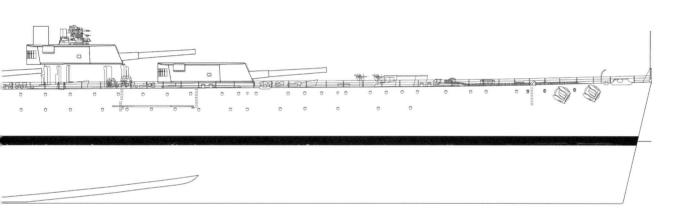

Top view

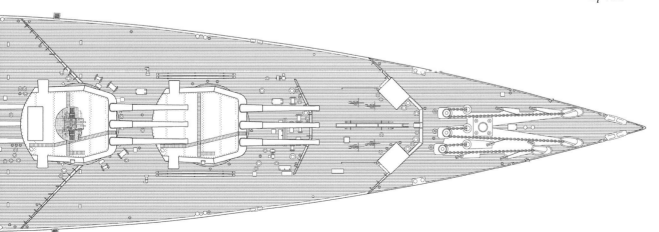

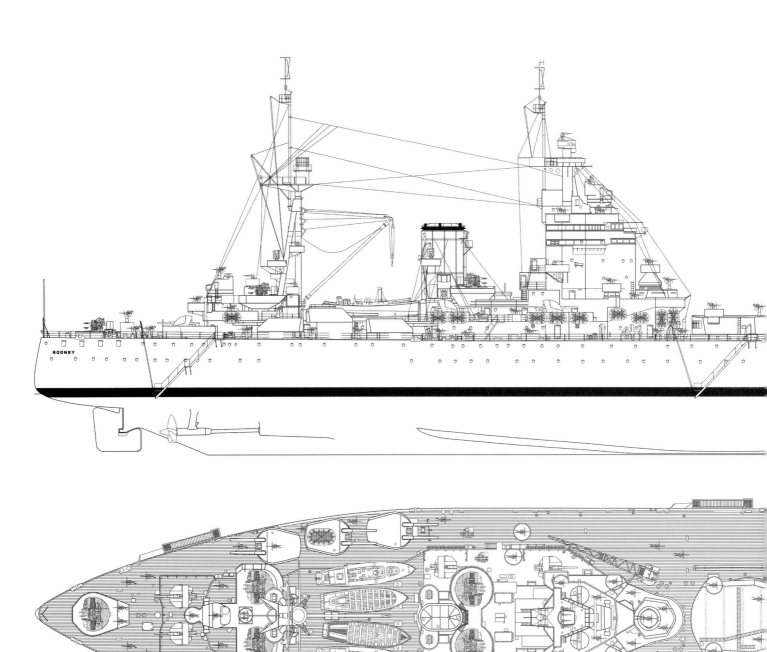

General arrangements HMS *Rodney* 1944.

1/550 scale

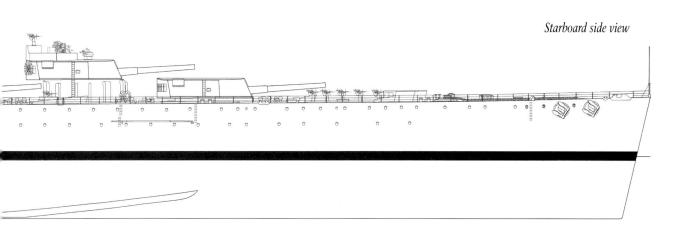

Starboard side view

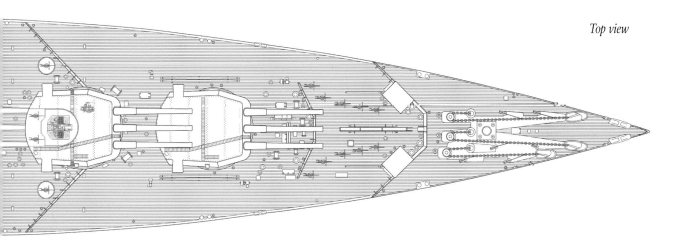

Top view

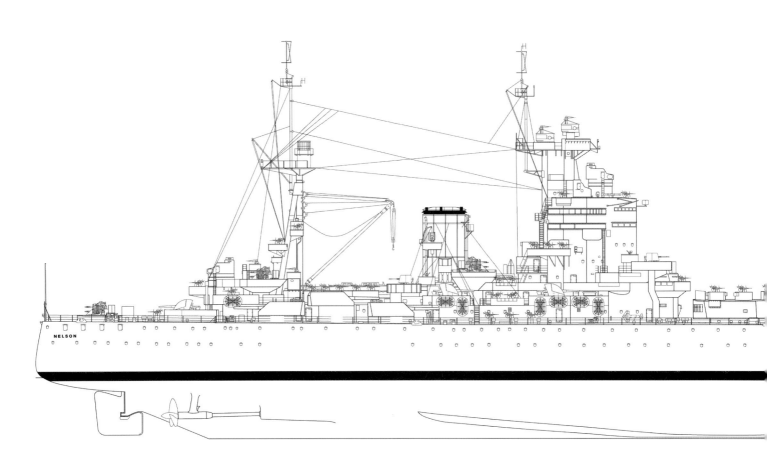

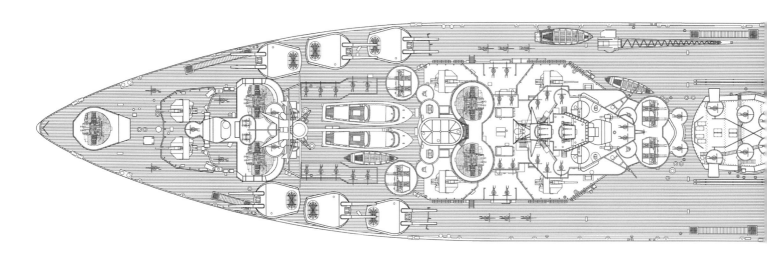

General arrangements HMS *Nelson* 1945.

1/550 scale

Starboard side view

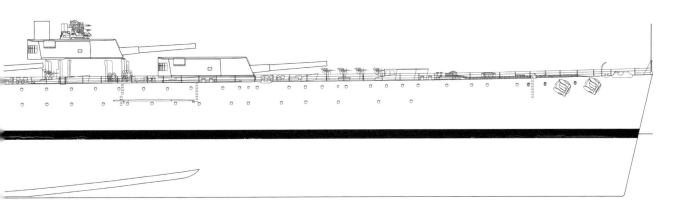

Top view

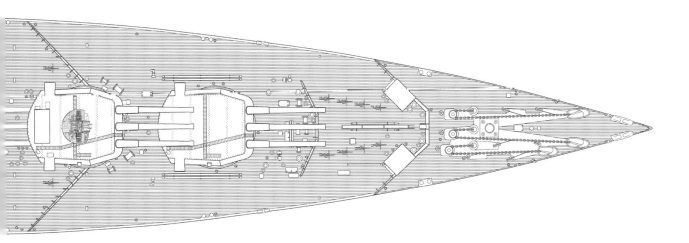

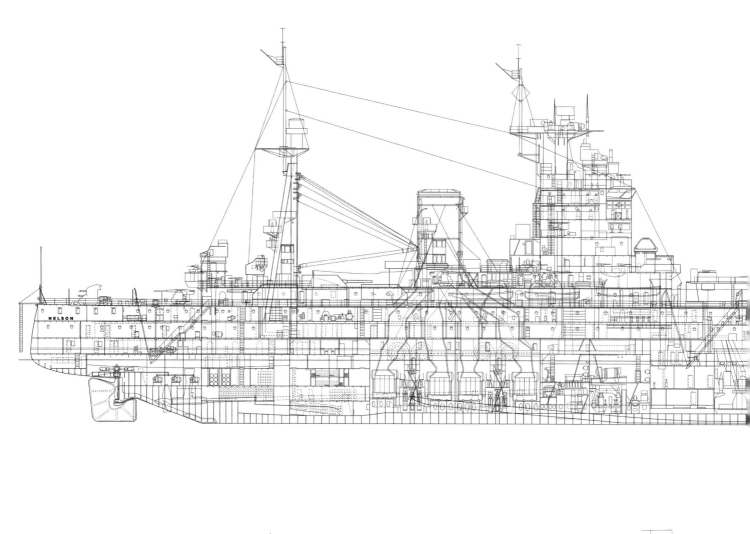

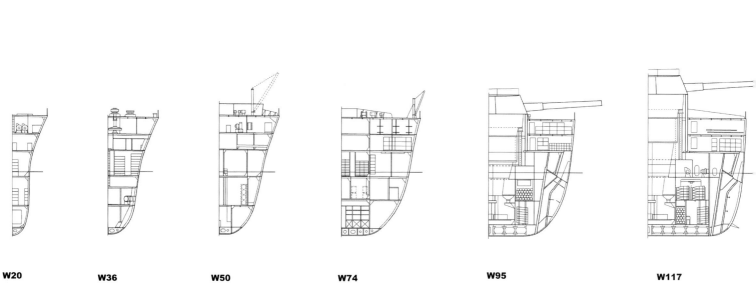

W20   **W36**   **W50**   **W74**   **W95**   **W117**

HMS *Nelson* profile (as fitted).

1/550 scale

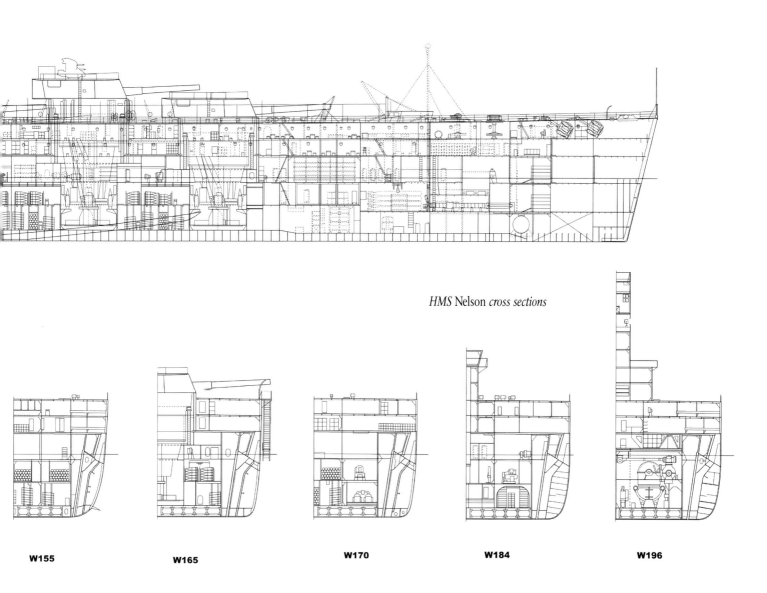

HMS Nelson *cross sections*

W155　　　**W165**　　　**W170**　　　**W184**　　　**W196**

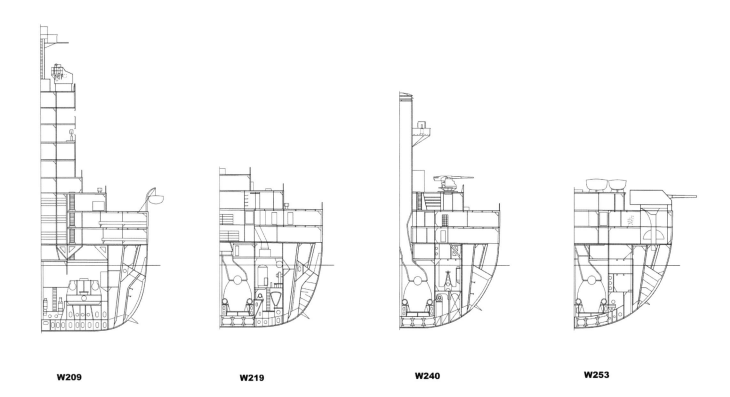

W209   W219   W240   W253

HMS Nelson *cross sections*

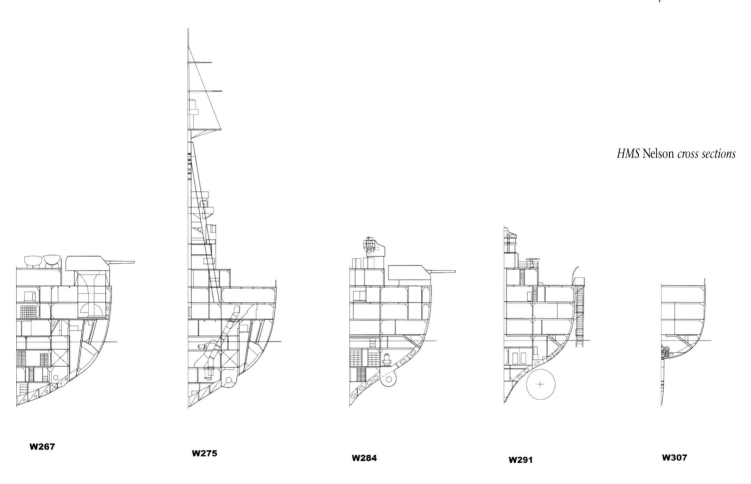

W267

W275

W284

W291

W307

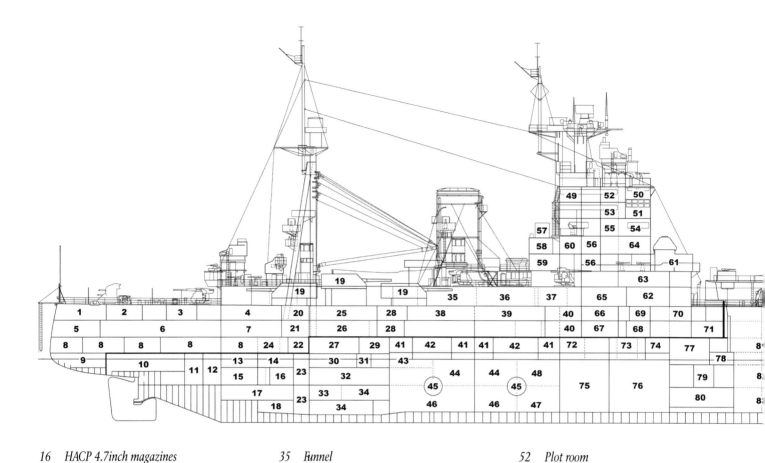

16 HACP 4.7inch magazines	35 Funnel	52 Plot room
17 4.7inch magazine	36 Bakery	53 Chart house
18 Watertight compartment	37 Ship's galley ready use flour store	54 Admiral's sea cabin
19 6 inch twin port & starboard	38 Gun room port	55 Radar workshop port
20 Type 282 radar office	39 Engineer's workshop port	56 Cabin port & starboard
21 No.3 DC HQ	40 Cook's lobby	57 RDF office
22 Radar power room	41 Uptake	58 Type 79 radar office
23 Feed water tank	42 Fan chamber port & starboard	59 Optical workshop starboard
24 Low power room	43 Engineer's tube store port & starboard	60 WC
25 Gun room baths & WCs port	44 Dynamo & evaporators room port & starboard	61 Conning tower
26 Main naval store	45 Boiler room	62 Victualling office
27 Main W/T office	46 Shaft passage port & starboard	63 Ready use store
28 Lobby	47 Auxiliary machinery compartments port & starboard 1	64 Officers' dormitory
29 Cypher office CO2 machinery	48 Auxiliary machinery compartments port & starboard 2	65 Laundry
30 Hoist compartment		66 Marines' mess port & starboard
31 Gyro room	49 Type 285 radar office	67 Stokers' drying room
32 6 inch shell room	50 Admiral's bridge	68 RM store
33 Handing room port & starboard /6 inch magazine	51 Compass platform	69 Victualling issue room
34 6 inch magazine		70 Mail office

1 Admiral's day cabin
2 Admiral's dining cabin
3 Admiral's pantry
4 Captain's accommodation cabin starboard.
5 Staff office
6 Cabins port & starboard
7 Cabin port church starboard
8 Cabins port & starboard

9 Provision room
10 Steering gear compartments
11 40 mm magazines
12 40 mm magazines/pump room starboard
13 Spirit room/provision stores
14 40 mm magazines port/20 mm magazines starboard
15 Spirit room port/pom-pom magazines

HMS *Nelson* general arrangements.

1/550 scale

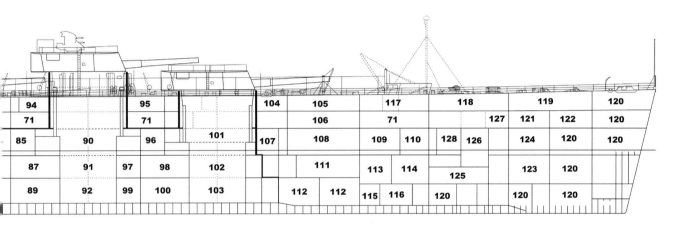

71 Seamen's mess port & starboard
72 Gun sight store port
73 20 & 40 magazines
74 Engineer's store port
75 Gearing room
76 Engine room
77 Radar power room port
78 LP generator room port & starboard
79 Dynamo rooms no. 3 & 4
80 4.7 magazines starboard
81 'X' turret barbette
82 'X' turret shell room port & starboard
83 'X' turret magazine port & starboard
84 Gyro compass room
85 Spare armature store port & starboard
86 'X' turret shell room
87 'B' turret shell room
88 'X' turret magazine

89 'B' turret magazine
90 'B' turret barbette
91 'B' turret shell room port & starboard
92 'B' turret magazine
93 Cooks/stewards' pantry & etc.
94 POs' pantry
95 Canteen
96 CO2 machinery compartment port
97 'B' turret shell room
98 'A' turret shell room
99 'B' turret magazine
100 'A' turret magazine
101 'A' turret barbette
102 'B' turret shell room
103 'B' turret magazine port & starboard
104 Reading room port
105 General reading room
106 Reading room/seamen's mess

107 Lobby
108 Provision room
109 Prisons port
110 Fresh water tanks
111 Cold &cool rooms
112 Naval store
113 Officers' baggage store
114 Awning store
115 Pump room
116 Fresh water tank
117 Shipwright's workshop port
118 Capstan machinery compartment
119 Seamen's heads
120 Water-tight compartments
121 Paint room
122 Cable gear store
123 Inflammable liquid store

HMS *Nelson* upper deck (as fitted).

1/550 scale

1   4.7inch HA mountings
2   6 inch twin port & starboard
3   6 inch barbette
4   Anteroom
5   Wardroom
6   Funnel
7   Passage
8   Ship's galley
9   Man kitchen
10 Bakery
11 Crane
12 'X' turret
13 'B' turret gun barbette
14 'A' turret

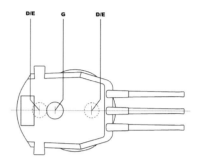

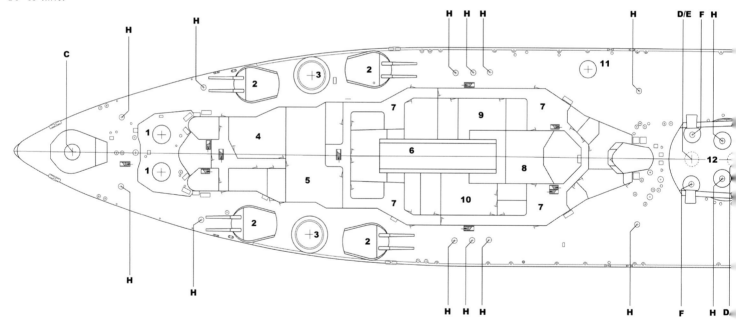

HMS *Nelson* upper deck (as fitted).

1/550 scale

Anti-aircraft armament alterations
1939
C   *One 40 mm pom-pom fitted*
D   *Two 178 mm U.P. projectors fitted*
1942
E   *Two 178 mm U.P. projectors removed*
F   *Three 20 mm Oerlikon guns fitted*
1943
H   *Eighteen 20 mm Oerlikon guns fitted*
1945
J   *Eight 20 mm Oerlikon guns fitted*

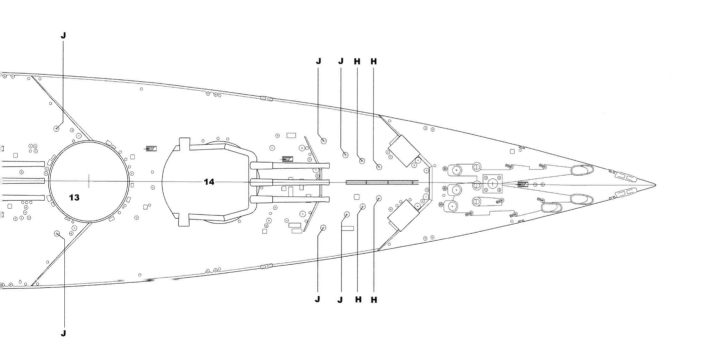

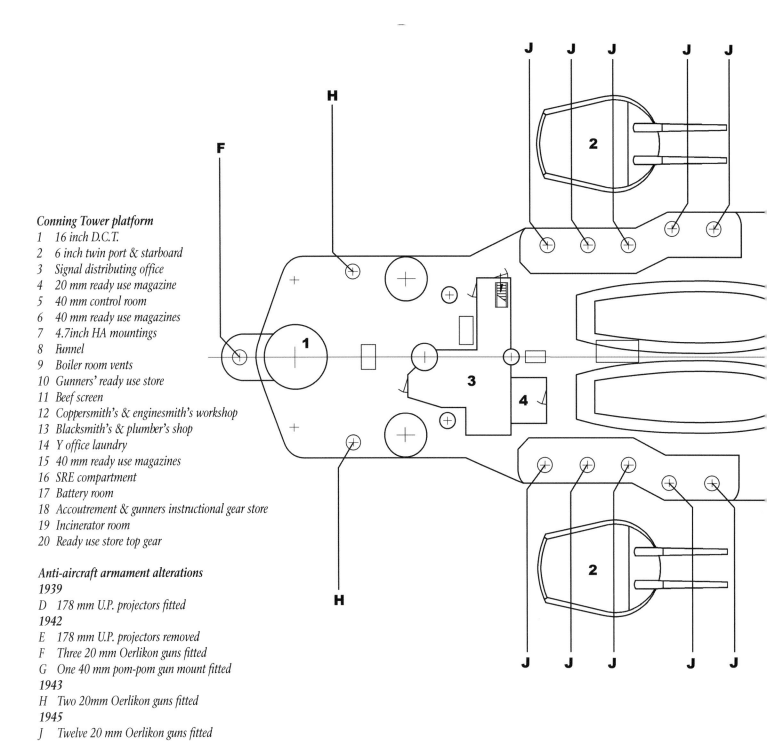

Conning Tower platform

1   16 inch D.C.T.
2   6 inch twin port & starboard
3   Signal distributing office
4   20 mm ready use magazine
5   40 mm control room
6   40 mm ready use magazines
7   4.7inch HA mountings
8   Funnel
9   Boiler room vents
10   Gunners' ready use store
11   Beef screen
12   Coppersmith's & enginesmith's workshop
13   Blacksmith's & plumber's shop
14   Y office laundry
15   40 mm ready use magazines
16   SRE compartment
17   Battery room
18   Accoutrement & gunners instructional gear store
19   Incinerator room
20   Ready use store top gear

Anti-aircraft armament alterations
1939
D   178 mm U.P. projectors fitted
1942
E   178 mm U.P. projectors removed
F   Three 20 mm Oerlikon guns fitted
G   One 40 mm pom-pom gun mount fitted
1943
H   Two 20mm Oerlikon guns fitted
1945
J   Twelve 20 mm Oerlikon guns fitted

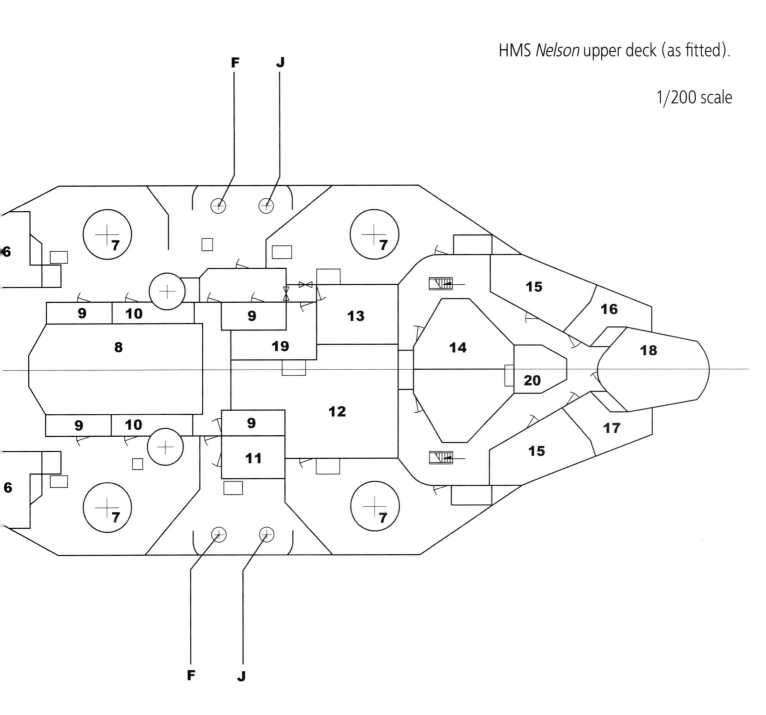

HMS *Nelson* upper deck (as fitted).

1/200 scale

1/200 scale

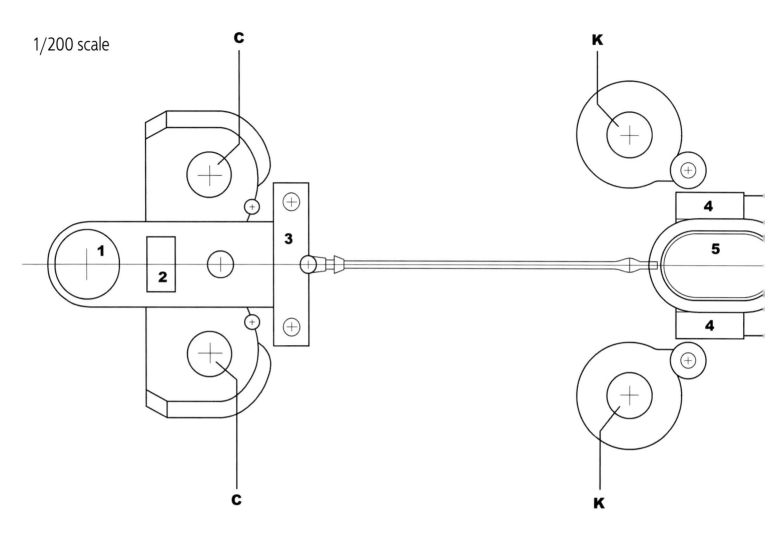

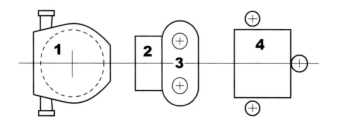

Director platform
1   16 inch D.C.T.
2   Shelter
3   6 inch barrage directors
4   Type 79 radar trang. office

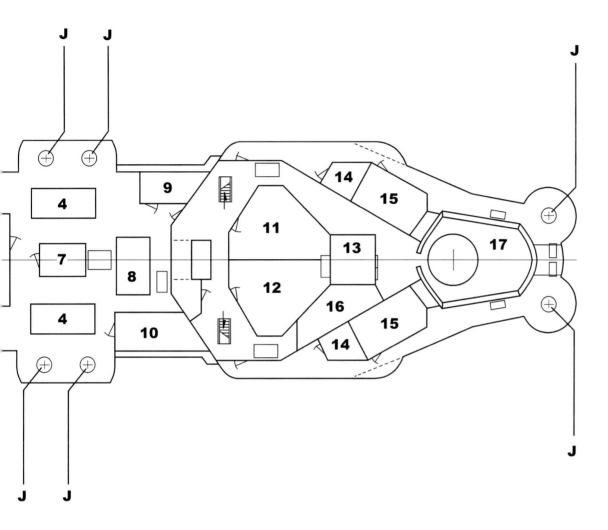

Conning tower platform
1. 16 inch D.C.T.
2. Shelter
3. Boat store
4. Boiler room vents
5. Funnel
6. 2. pom-pom ready use magazines
7. 20 mm ready use magazines
8. Vegetable locker
9. Ship's heads
10. Optical workshop
11. Cabin no. 76
12. Cabin no. 75
13. V/S office
14. 40 mm control room
15. 40 mm ready use magazines
16. Meteorological office
17. Upper conning tower

Anti-aircraft armament alterations
1939
C Two 40 mm pom-pom gun mounts fitted
1945
J Six 20 mm Oerlikon guns fitted
K Two 40 mm Bofors gun mounts fitted

Admirals bridge
1. Type 285 radar office
2. R.C. position
3. Strategical & air plot.
4. Admiral's bridge

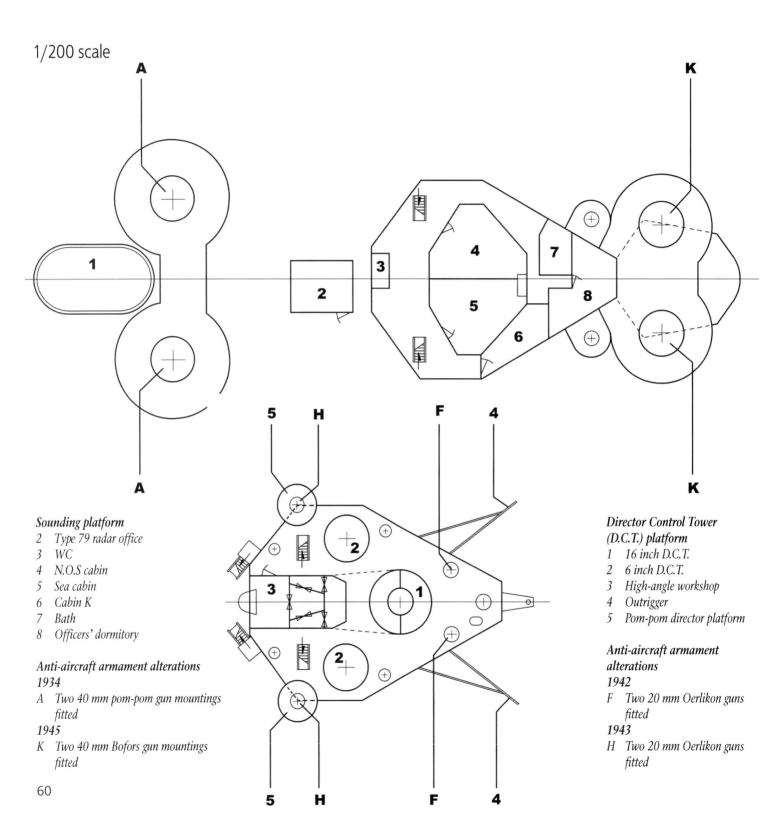

1/200 scale

Sounding platform
2 Type 79 radar office
3 WC
4 N.O.S cabin
5 Sea cabin
6 Cabin K
7 Bath
8 Officers' dormitory

Anti-aircraft armament alterations
1934
A Two 40 mm pom-pom gun mountings
   fitted
1945
K Two 40 mm Bofors gun mountings
   fitted

**Director Control Tower
(D.C.T.) platform**
1 16 inch D.C.T.
2 6 inch D.C.T.
3 High-angle workshop
4 Outrigger
5 Pom-pom director platform

**Anti-aircraft armament
alterations**
1942
F Two 20 mm Oerlikon guns
   fitted
1943
H Two 20 mm Oerlikon guns
   fitted

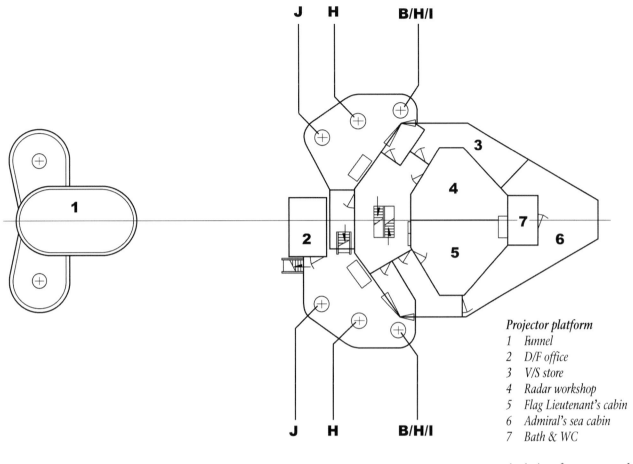

J   **H**   **B/H/I**

J   **H**   **B/H/I**

Projector platform
1   *Funnel*
2   *D/F office*
3   *V/S store*
4   *Radar workshop*
5   *Flag Lieutenant's cabin*
6   *Admiral's sea cabin*
7   *Bath & WC*

Anti-aircraft armament alterations
1935
B   *Two 12.7 mm Vickers machine*
    gun mountings fitted

1943
H   *Four 20 mm Oerlikon guns fitted*
I   *Two 12.7 mm Vickers machine*
    gun mountings removed

1945
J   *Two 20 mm Oerlikon guns fitted*

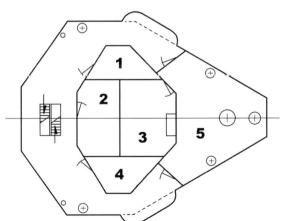

Captains bridge & compass platform
1   *Shelter*
2   *Captain's sea cabin*
3   *Chart house*
4   *R/T office*
5   *Compass platform*

1/200 scale

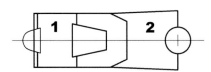

Support to air defence position
1   Type 285 radar office
2   Platform

Air defence position
1   High Angle director
2   A.L.O. sights port & starboard
3   A.L.O. sights port & starboard
4   Signalling lantern

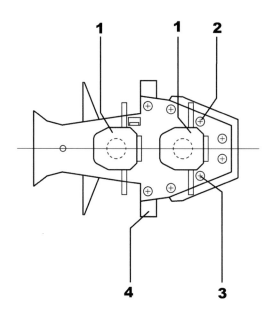

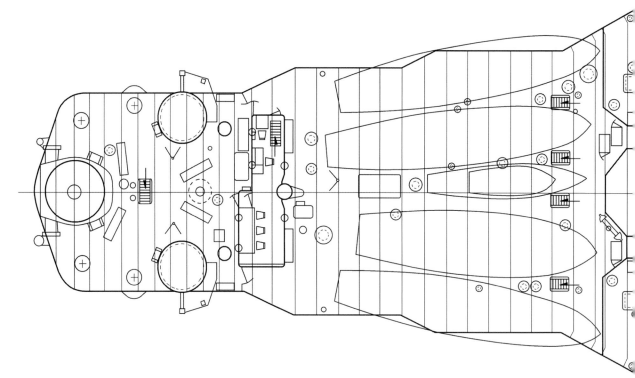

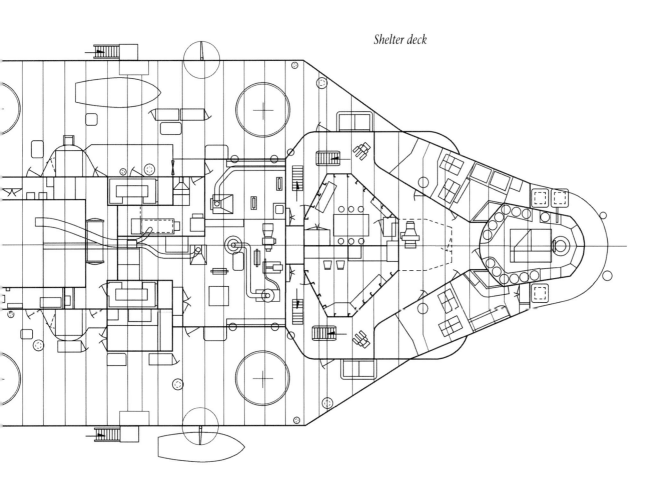

Shelter deck

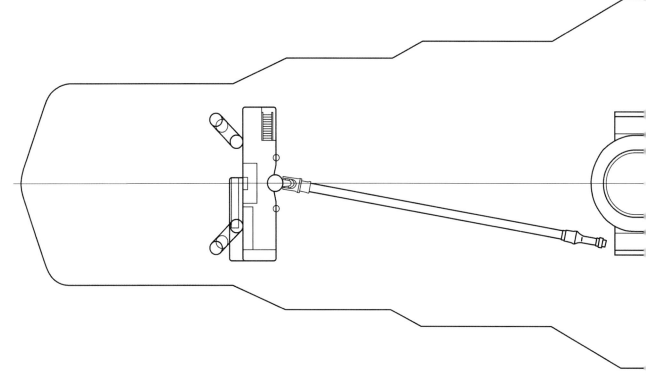

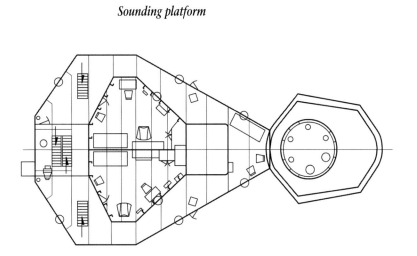

Sounding platform

Forward searchlight manipulating huts etc.

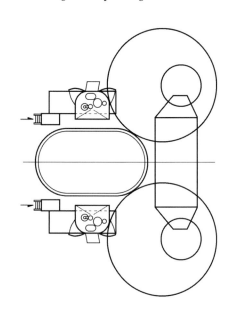

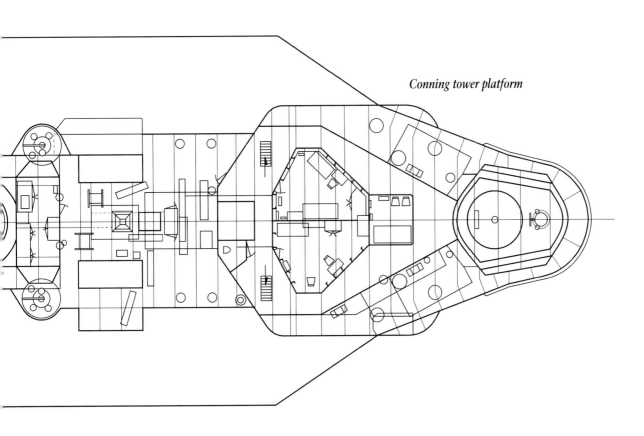

Conning tower platform

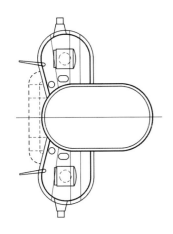

Searchlight platforms on funnel

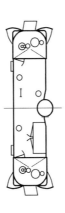

After searchlight manipulating huts

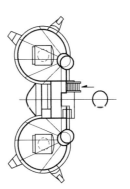

Searchlight platform on mast

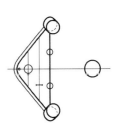

1-metre rangefinder platform

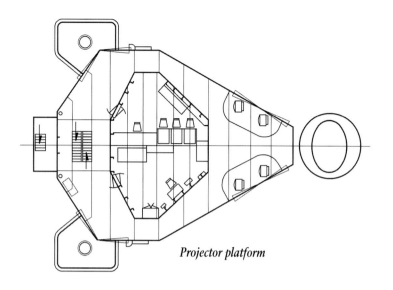

Projector platform

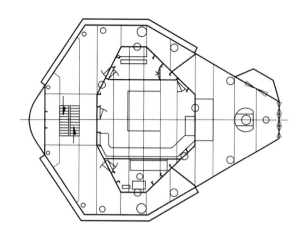

Captain's bridge & compass platform

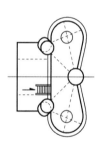

Pom-pom control

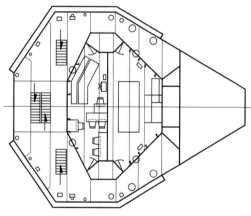

Admiral's bridge

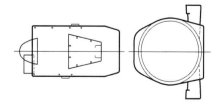

D.C.T. etc.

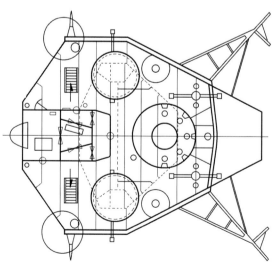

D.C.T. platform

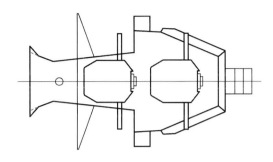

High Angle control platform

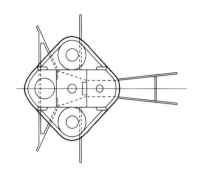

High Angle control platform (later removed)

Not to scale

Simplified armour layout cross section at turret B.

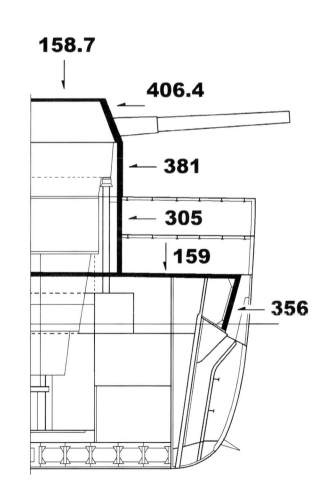

Simplified armour layout vertical cross section

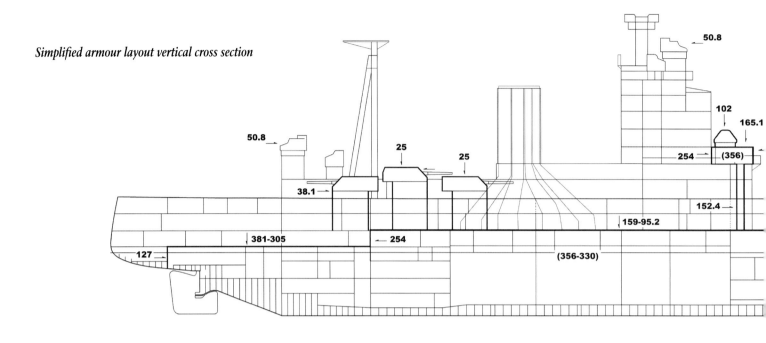

Simplified armour layout horizontal cross section

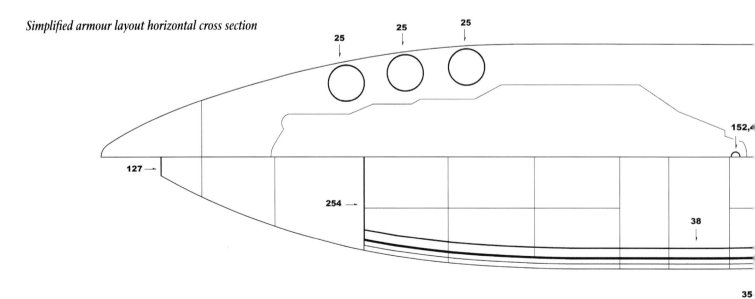

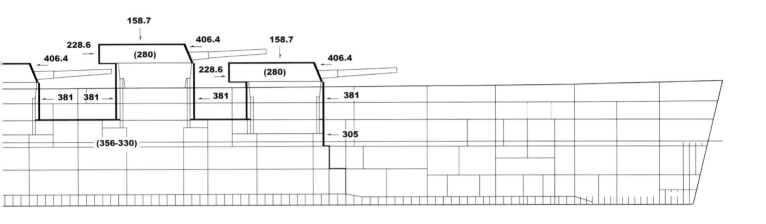

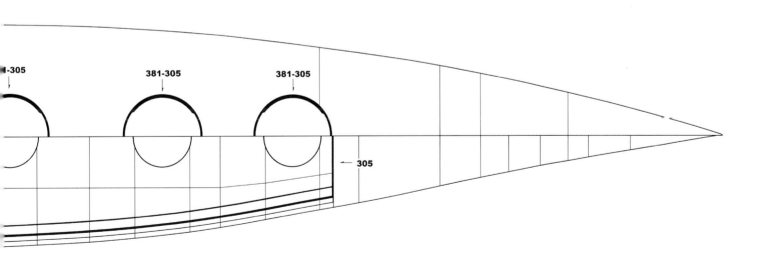

Not to scale

General arrangements of engine rooms

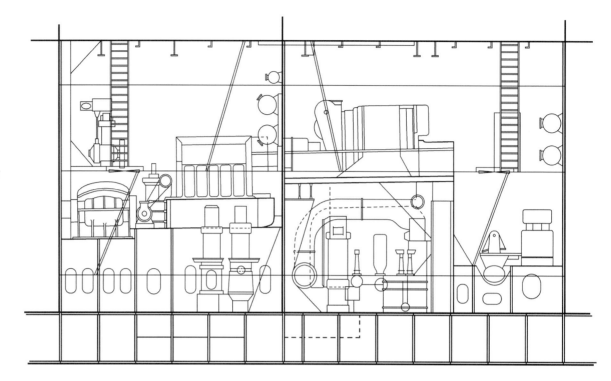

General arrangements of boiler rooms

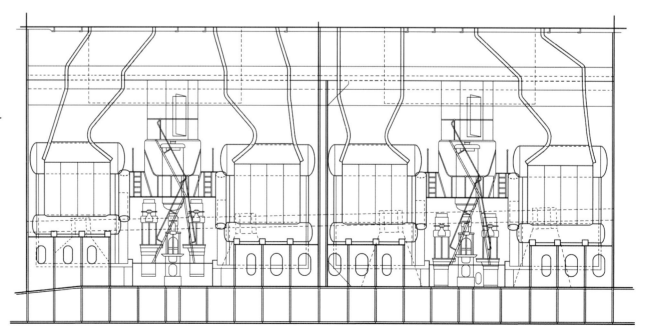

Main anchor gear, profile
1 Mooring bollard
2 Cable holder brake handle
3 Cable holder
4 Cable holder spindle
5 Capstan
6 Worm wheel drive to spindles
7 Cable locker
8 Clump cathead, port and starboard
9 Anchor
10 Towing fairlead

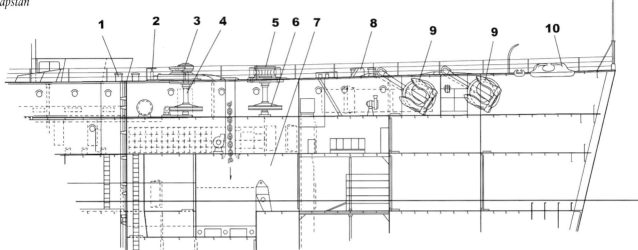

Main anchor gear plan
1 Mooring bollard
2 Cable holder brake handle
3 Cable holder
4 Navel pipes with water-tight bonnet
5 Rollers
6 Capstan
7 Eye plates
8 Hatch and ladderway to heads
9 Clump cathead, port and starboard
10 Anchor
11 Hinged hawse pipe cover
12 Towing fairlead

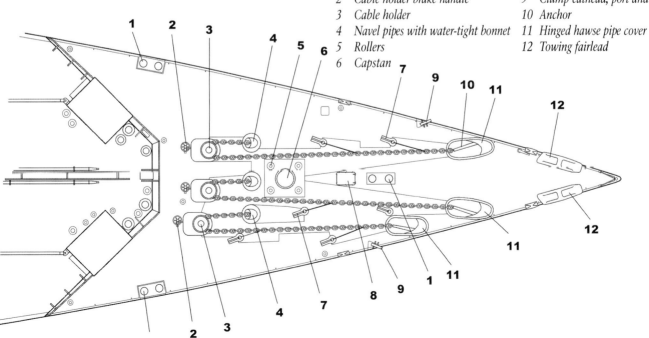

Not to scale

Quarterdeck

1 Towing fairlead
2 Bollards
3 Multiple 2 Pdr 1.6in (40 mm) AA guns
4 Wood gratings
5 Ladder and platform working davit
6 Warp boom
7 Ensign staff
8 4.7in (120 mm) AA guns
9 Capstan

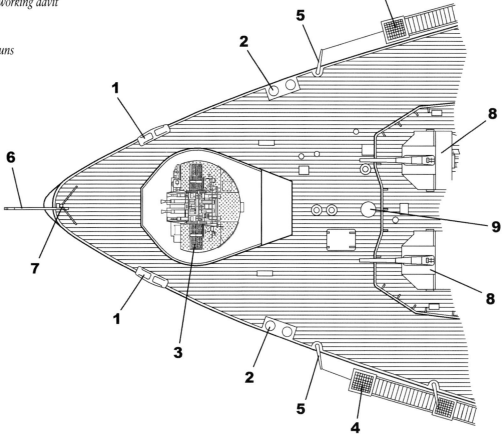

Not to scale

Bow structure
1 Towing fairlead
2 Upper deck
3 Main deck
4 Middle deck
5 Lower deck
6 Platform deck
7 Channel bar deck beams
8 Angle bulb deck beams
9 Floor plates
10 Vertical keel

Stern structure
1 Upper deck
2 Main deck
3 Middle deck
4 Lower deck
5 Centre-line of rudder
6 Floor plates
7 Non water-tight vertical keel
8 Rudder bedding
9 Stern casting

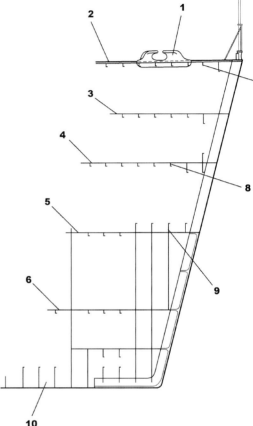

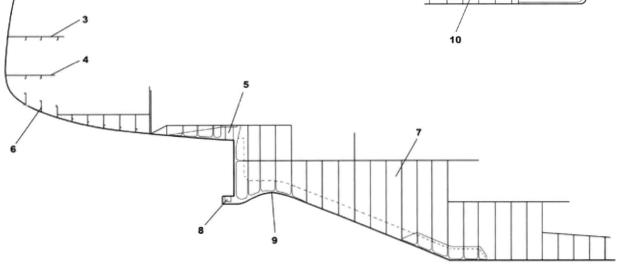

73

1/200 scale

Superstructure HMS Rodney *1928*

1 HA control platform
2 6in D.C.T.
3 16 inch D.C.T.
4 Admiral's bridge
5 Signaling projector
6 Saluting gun
7 120 mm gun
8 40 mm gun
9 Conning tower

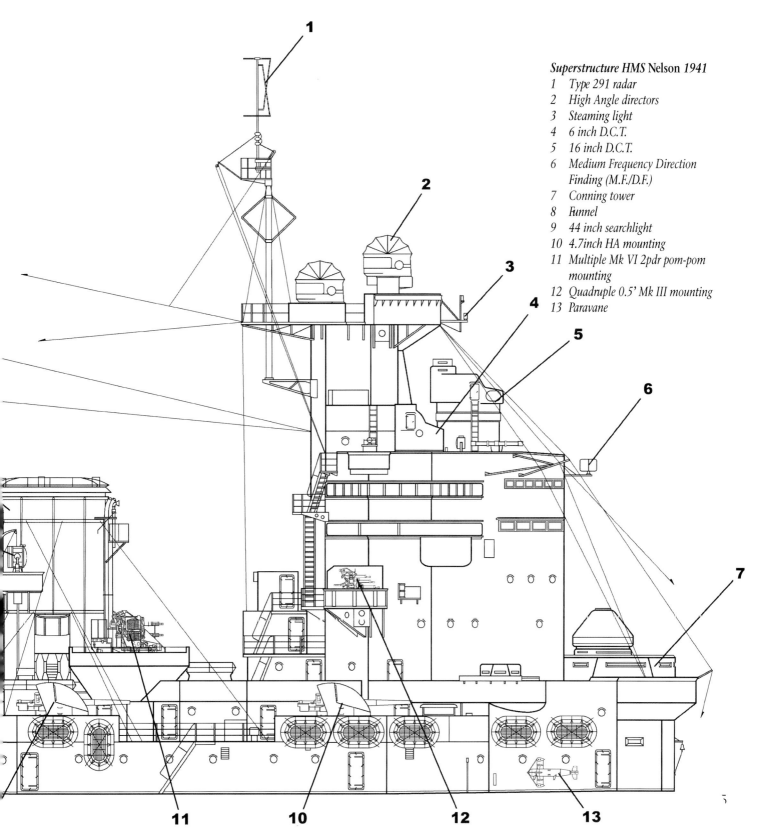

Superstructure HMS Nelson 1941

1   Type 291 radar
2   High Angle directors
3   Steaming light
4   6 inch D.C.T.
5   16 inch D.C.T.
6   Medium Frequency Direction
    Finding (M.F./D.F.)
7   Conning tower
8   Funnel
9   44 inch searchlight
10 4.7inch HA mounting
11 Multiple Mk VI 2pdr pom-pom
    mounting
12 Quadruple 0.5' Mk III mounting
13 Paravane

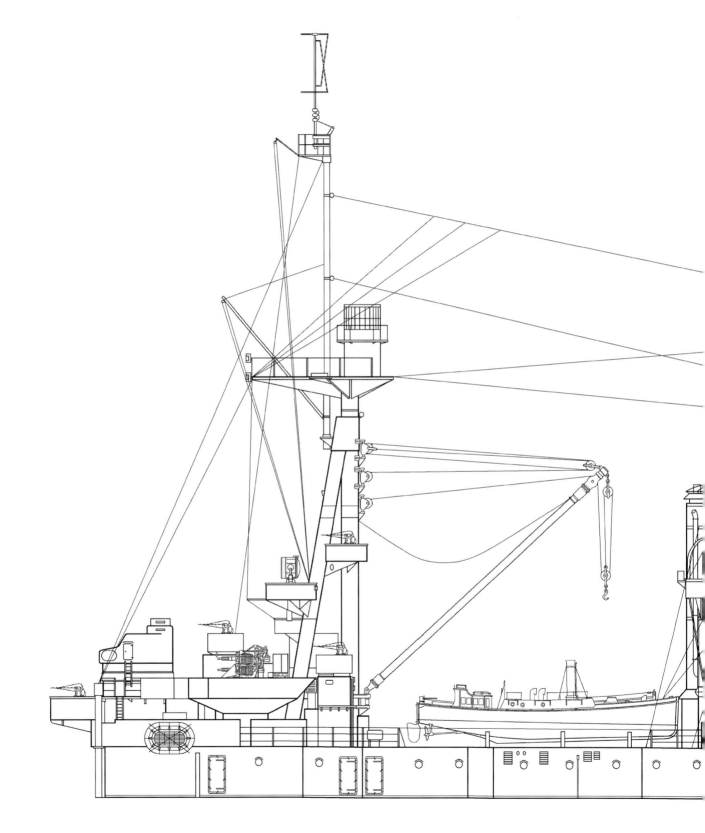

Superstructure HMS Rodney *1942*

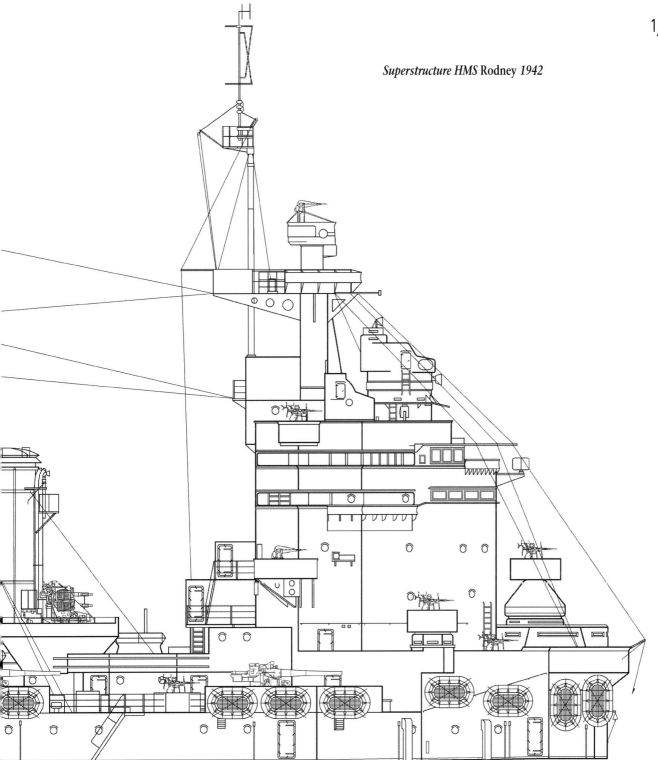

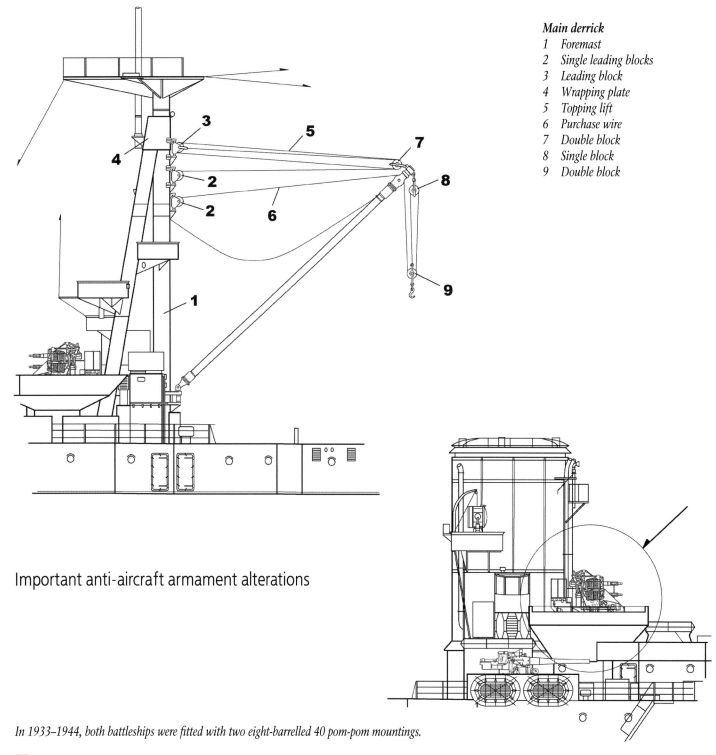

Main derrick
1 Foremast
2 Single leading blocks
3 Leading block
4 Wrapping plate
5 Topping lift
6 Purchase wire
7 Double block
8 Single block
9 Double block

Important anti-aircraft armament alterations

In 1933–1944, both battleships were fitted with two eight-barrelled 40 pom-pom mountings.

Important anti-aircraft armament alterations
1/200 scale

In 1934–1935, both battleships were fitted with two four-barrelled 12.7 mm anti-aircraft machine gun mountings.

In 1939, Nelson *received an additional 40 mm pom-pom gun mounting, which was fitted in place of the aft fire control towers (as did* Rodney*).*

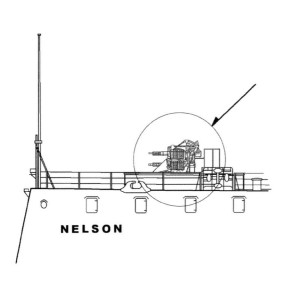

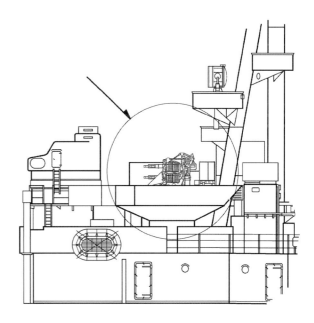

In 1939, Nelson *was fitted with additional 40 mm pom-pom gun mounting (as was* Rodney*).*

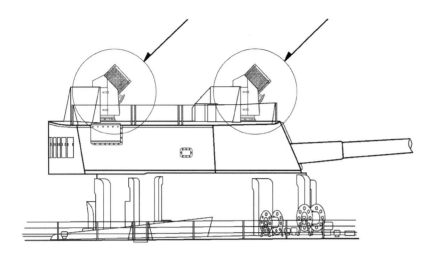

In 1939, Nelson *was fitted with four UP (Unrotated Projectile) projectors.*

Between October 1941 and March 1942, Nelson *received additional eight-barrelled 40 mm pom-pom gun mountings fitted in place of the removed U.P. projector on the roof of 'B' turret (in the case of* Rodney, *the mounting was a four-barrelled variant).*

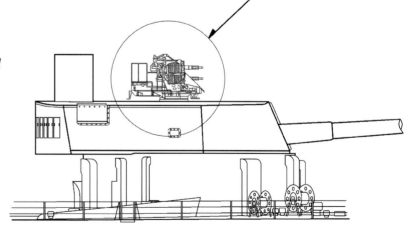

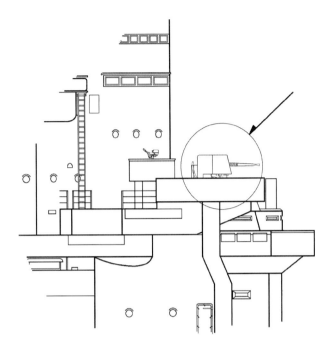

Between September 1944 and January 1945, Nelson received four additional four-barrelled 40 mm Bofors gun mountings, fitted in front of the conning tower.

Nelson received two additional 40 mm Bofors gun mountings fitted behind the funnel.

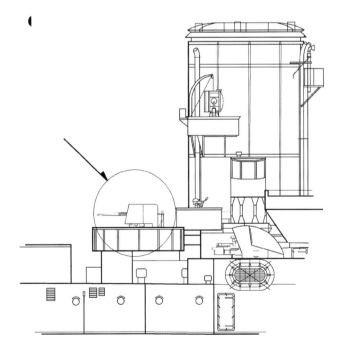

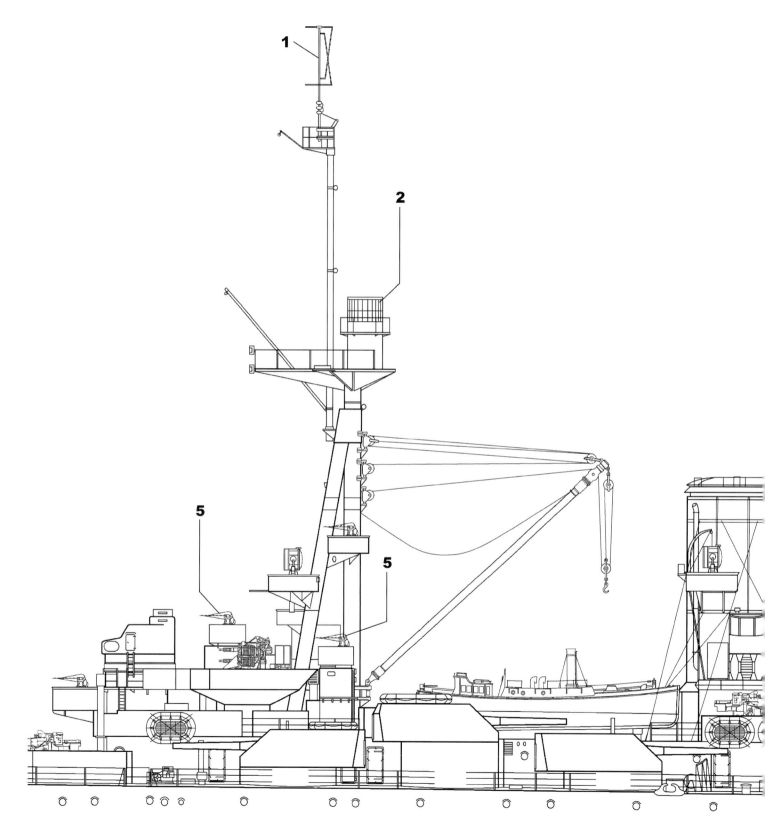

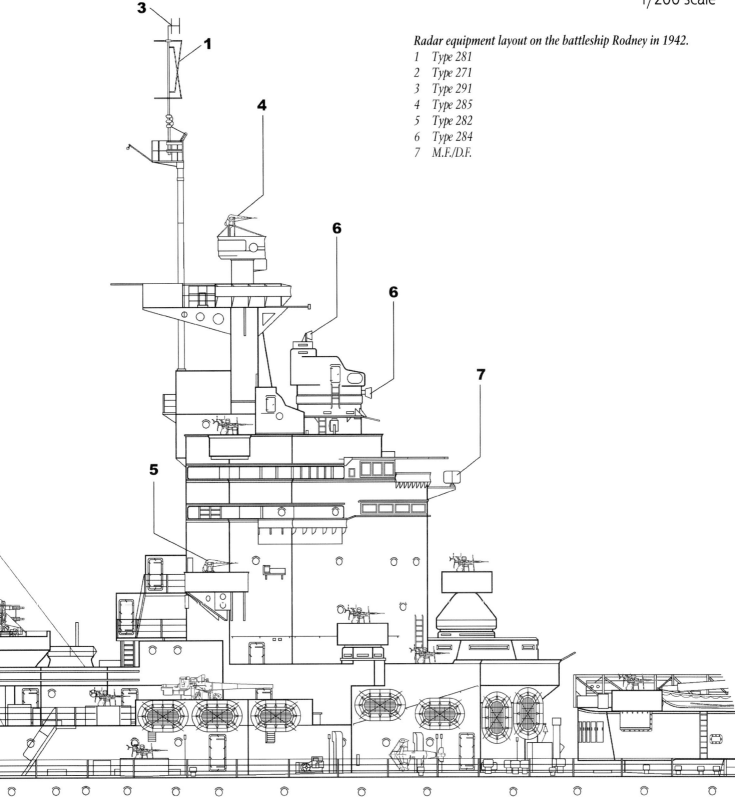

1/200 scale

Radar equipment layout on the battleship Rodney in 1942.
1   Type 281
2   Type 271
3   Type 291
4   Type 285
5   Type 282
6   Type 284
7   M.F./D.F.

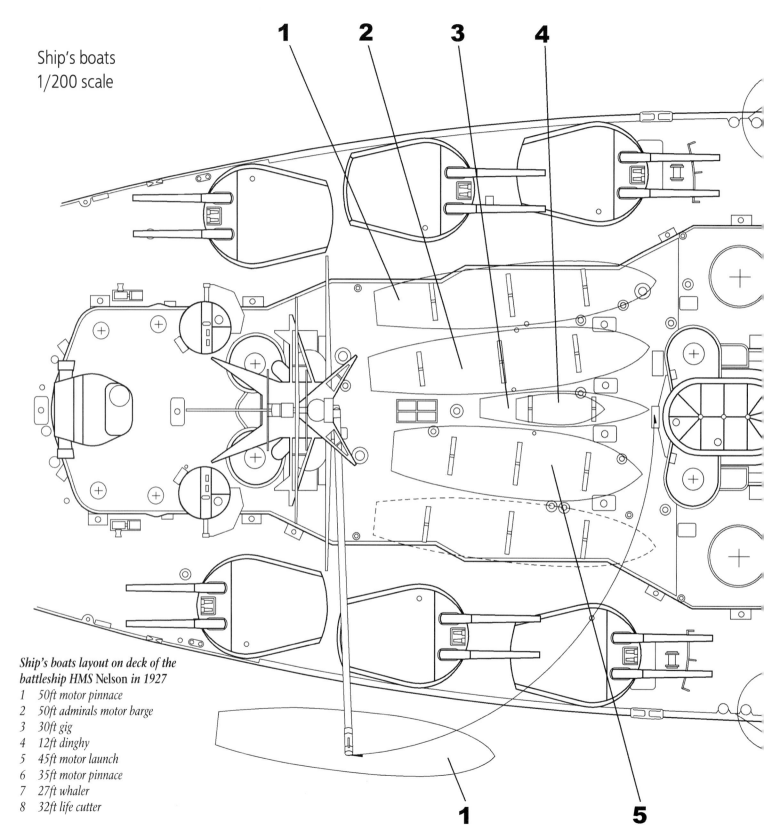

Ship's boats
1/200 scale

Ship's boats layout on deck of the
battleship HMS Nelson in 1927

1   *50ft motor pinnace*
2   *50ft admirals motor barge*
3   *30ft gig*
4   *12ft dinghy*
5   *45ft motor launch*
6   *35ft motor pinnace*
7   *27ft whaler*
8   *32ft life cutter*

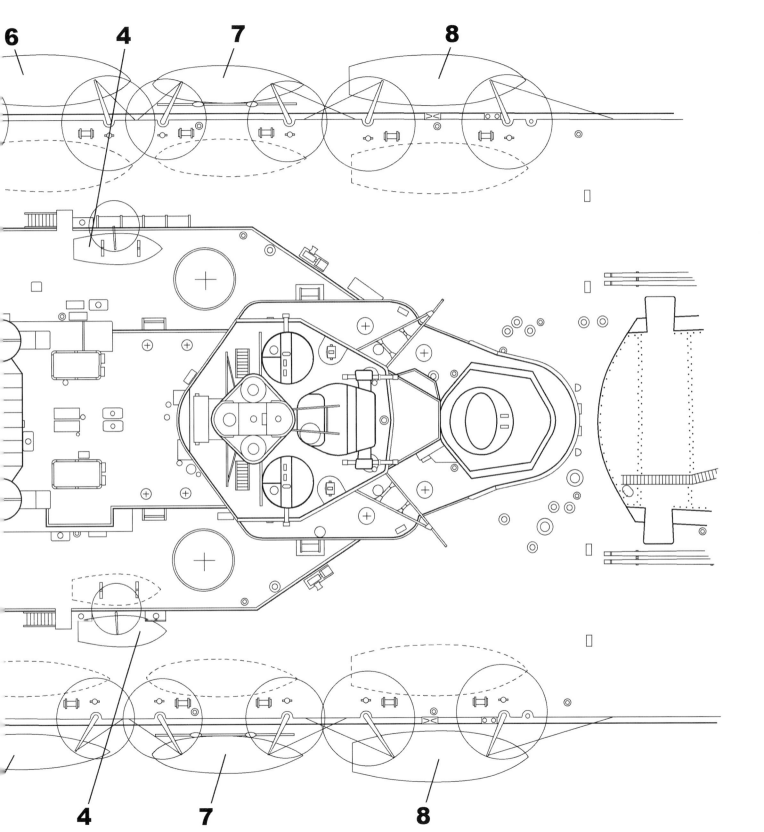

1/200 scale

50ft steam pinnace

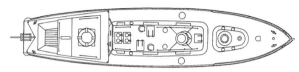

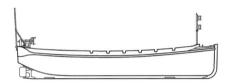

36ft pinnace

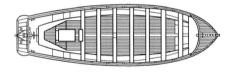

30ft gig

16ft sailing dinghy

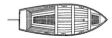

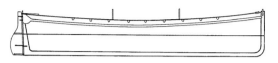

42ft sailing launch

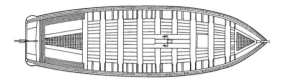

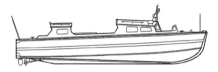

35ft fast motor boat

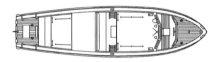

32ft cutter

Balsa raft

Triple 16in (406 mm) guns,
general view

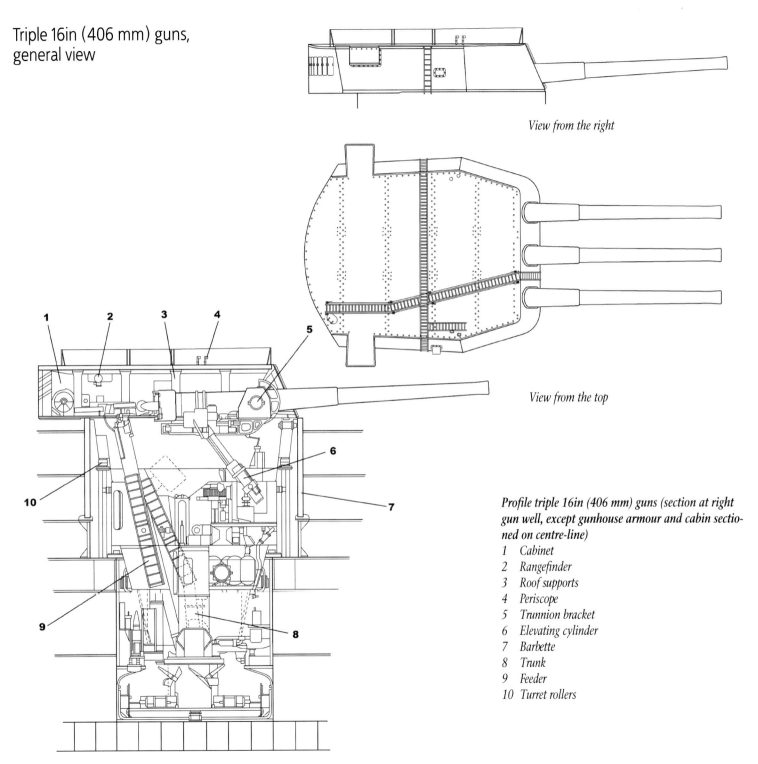

View from the right

View from the top

Profile triple 16in (406 mm) guns (section at right
gun well, except gunhouse armour and cabin sectio-
ned on centre-line)

1   Cabinet
2   Rangefinder
3   Roof supports
4   Periscope
5   Trunnion bracket
6   Elevating cylinder
7   Barbette
8   Trunk
9   Feeder
10 Turret rollers

87

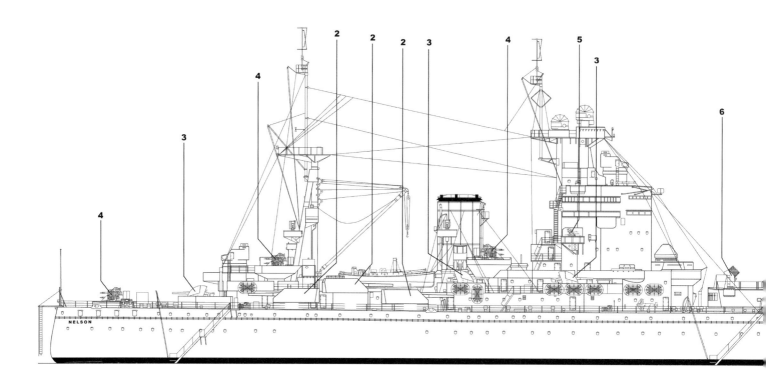

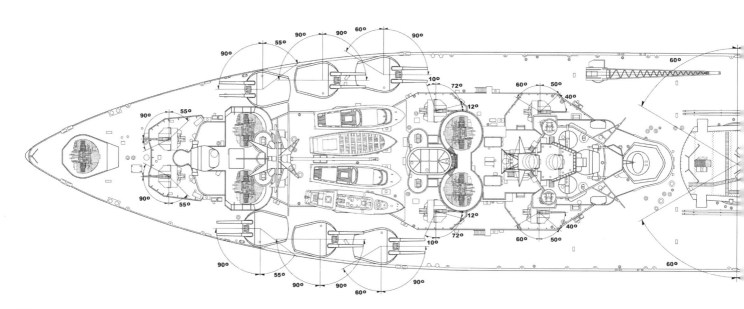

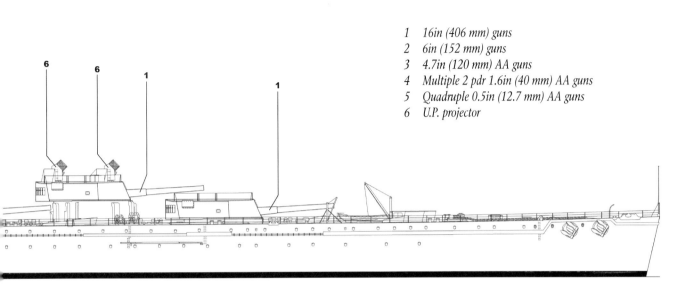

1   *16in (406 mm) guns*
2   *6in (152 mm) guns*
3   *4.7in (120 mm) AA guns*
4   *Multiple 2 pdr 1.6in (40 mm) AA guns*
5   *Quadruple 0.5in (12.7 mm) AA guns*
6   *U.P. projector*

Simplified shipboard weapons firing arcs diagram – battleship Nelson.

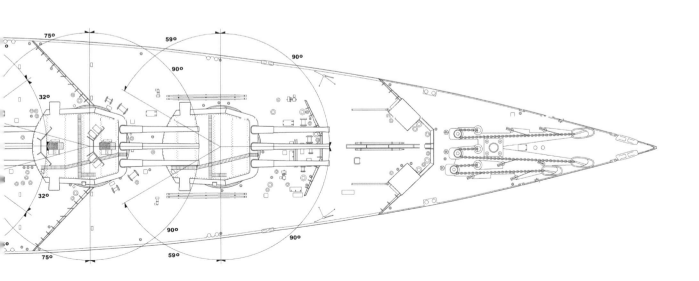

1/200 scale

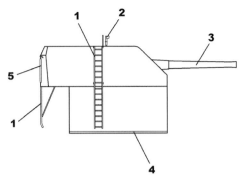

Twin 6in (152 mm) guns, general view
View from the right
1 Ladder
2 Periscope
3 Barrel
4 Barbette
5 Hatch

View from the left

View from the right

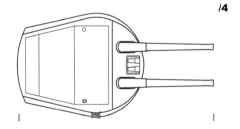

View from the top

Single 4.7in (120 mm) guns
View from the right
1 Trunnion
2 Gun trainer's sight
3 Vertical training shaft
4 Barrel
5 Gear
6 Pedestal
7 Training handles

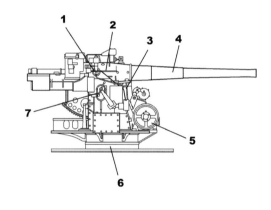

View from the left (shield)

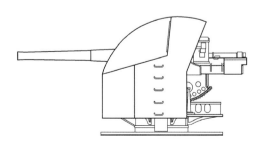

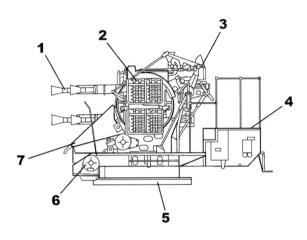

Eight-barrel 1.6in (40 mm) 2 pdr pom-pom mounting
View from the left
1   Flash guards
2   Ammunition feed boxes
3   Trainer's sight
4   Platform
5   Pedestal
6   Electric motor
7   Empty cartridge chute

View from the rear

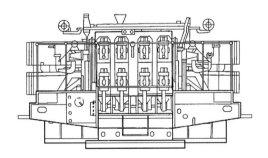

View from the front

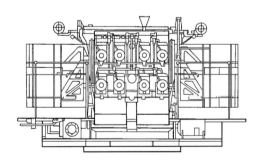

1/75 scale

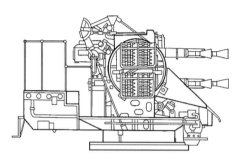

View from the right

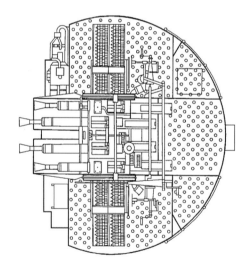

View from the top

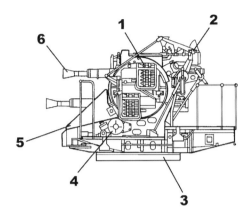

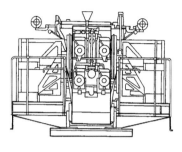

View from the front

Four-barrelled 1.6in (40 mm) 2pdr pom-pom mounting
View from the left

1 Ammunition feed boxes
2 Trainer's sight
3 Pedestal
4 Electric motor
5 Empty cartridge chute
6 Flash guards

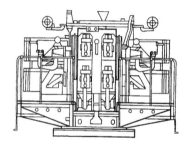

View from the rear

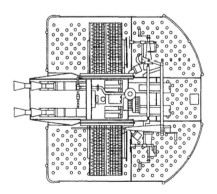

View from the top

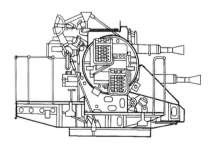

View from the right

1/50 scale

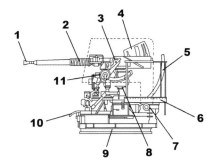

View from the front

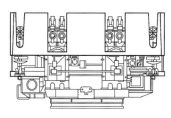

View from the right

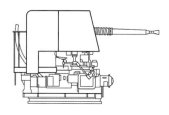

View from the left

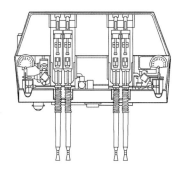

View from the top

Four-barrelled 40 mm Bofors mounting

1   Flash guards
2   Recoil springs
3   Trunnion
4   Outline of loader hood
5   Case discharge chutes

6   Platform
7   Cooling motor and pump
8   Pointer's seat
9   Pedestal
10   Case discharge chutes
11   Elevating crank

40 mm single Vickers on pedestal mounting

1   Barrel
2   Sight
3   Cooling sleeve
4   Elevation scale

5   Training handwheel
6   Footrest
7   Layer's seat
8   Breech

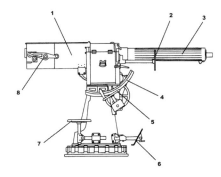

View from the right

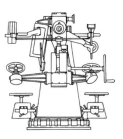

View from the front

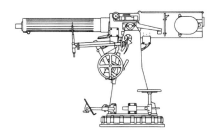

View from the left

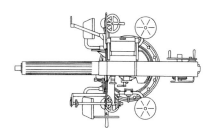

View from the top

1/50 scale

1/25 scale

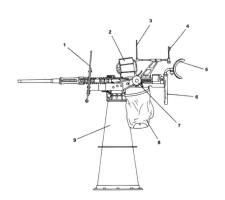

View from the left

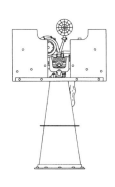

View from the front

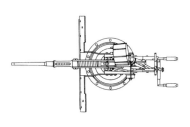

View from the top

20 mm single Oerlikon on pedestal mounting

1	Shield	4	Back sight	8	Cartridge bag
2	Magazine	5	Shoulder rests	9	Pedestal
3	Fore sight	6	Back strap		
		7	Elevation counter balance spring case		

1/75 scale

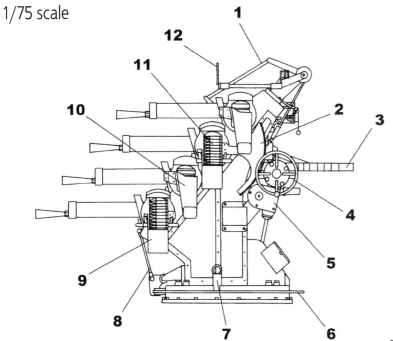

View from the left

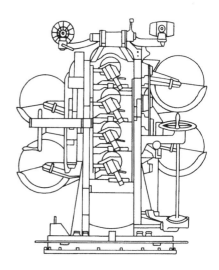

View from the front

Four-barrelled 0.5in (12.7 mm) mounting
1 Sight link motions
2 Elevation arc
3 Layer's body rest
4 Elevation handwheel
5 Elevation gearbox
6 Depression rail
7 Locking bolt
8 Depression control link and follower
9 Ammunition drum guard plate
10 Empty cartridge chute
11 Ammunition feed drums
12 Layer's open sight

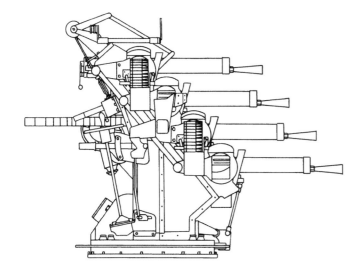

View from the right

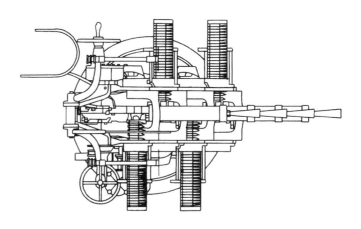

View from the top

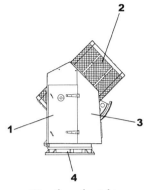 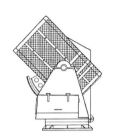  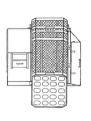 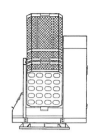

View from the right   *View from the left*   *View from the front*   *View from the top*   *View from the rear*

U.P. mounting
1   Mesh frame around tubes
2   Layer's cabinet
3   Door to layer's cabinet
4   Pedestal

1/50 scale

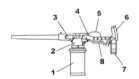 

View from the left   *View from the front*   *View from the top*

3 Pdr saluting gun
1   Pedestal
2   Carriage
3   Recoil cylinder
4   Run out spring
5   Sliding breech block
6   Shoulder rest
7   Hand grips
8   Firing pistol grip

Paravane

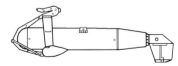

View from the left

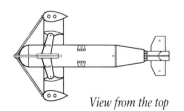

View from the top

97

1/100 scale

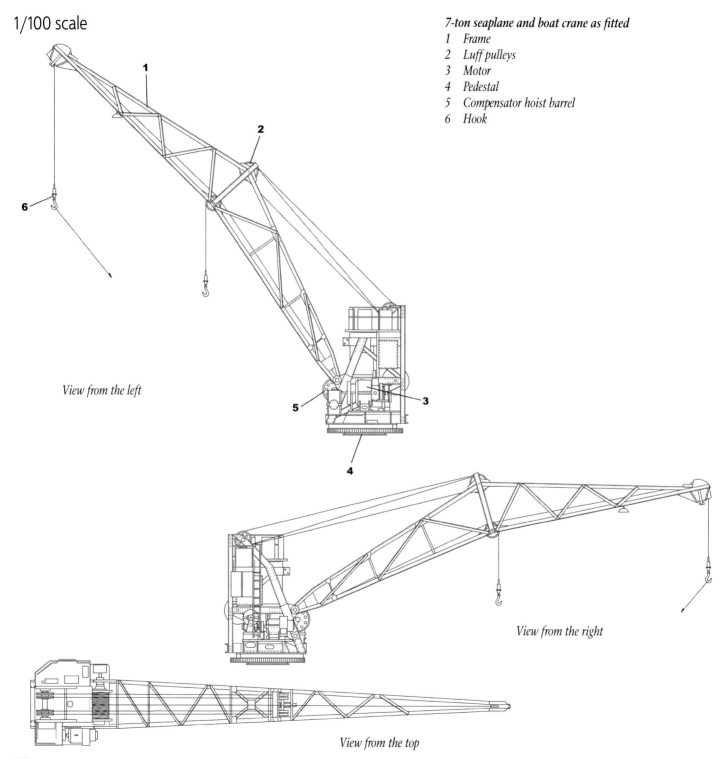

7-ton seaplane and boat crane as fitted
1 Frame
2 Luff pulleys
3 Motor
4 Pedestal
5 Compensator hoist barrel
6 Hook

View from the left

View from the right

View from the top

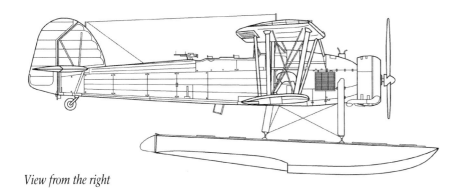

View from the right

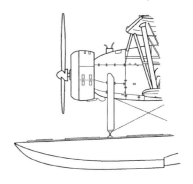

View from the left (engine section)

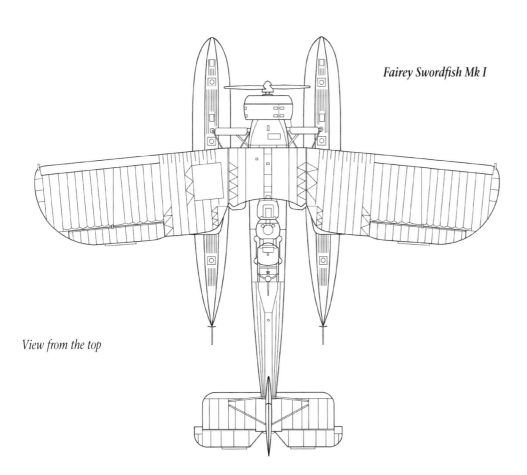

Fairey Swordfish Mk I

View from the top

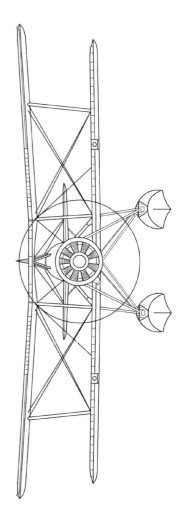

View from the front

1/100 scale

Supermarine Walrus Mk I

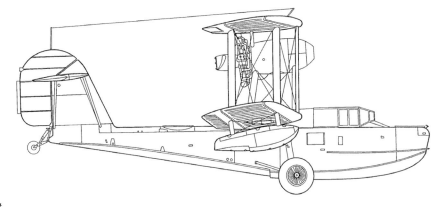

View from the right

View from the top

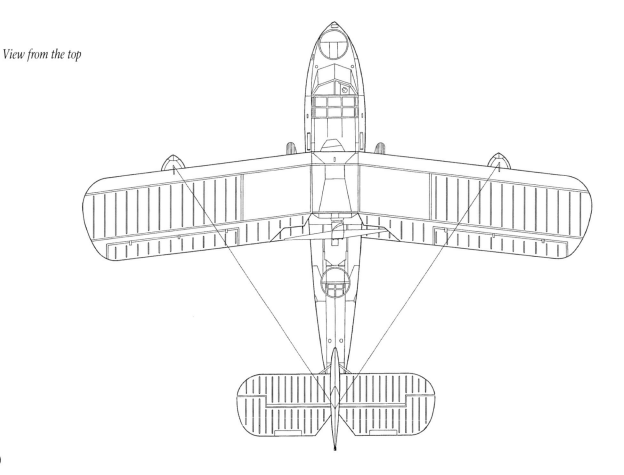

Supermarine Walrus Mk I

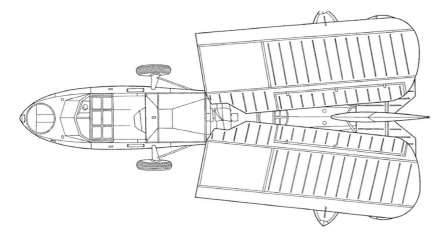

View from the top (folded wings)

View from the front

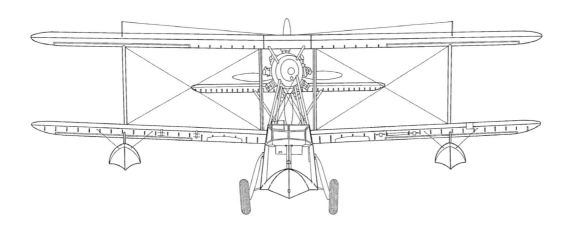

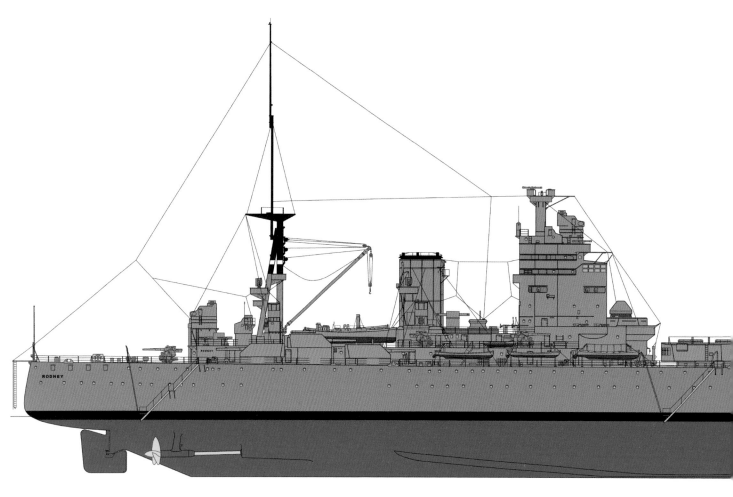

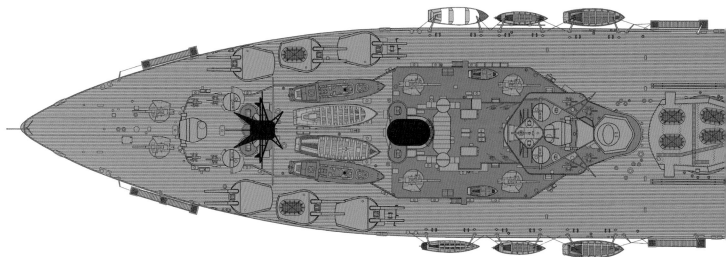

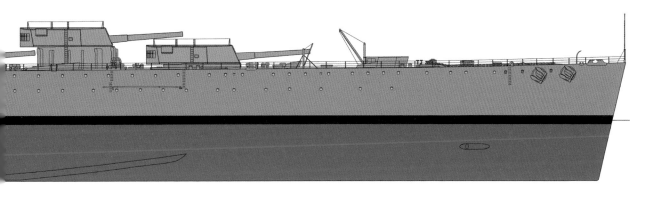

HMS Rodney in 1928 paint scheme

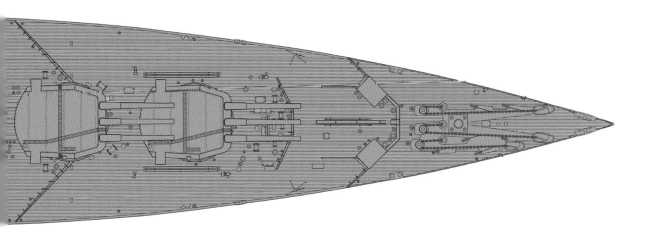

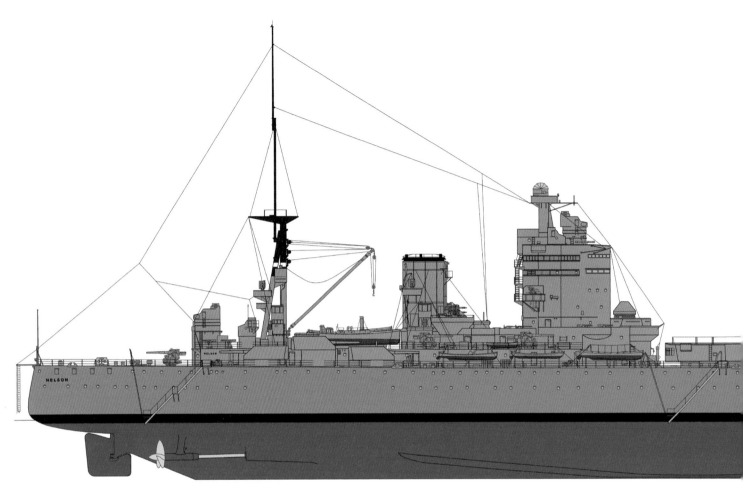

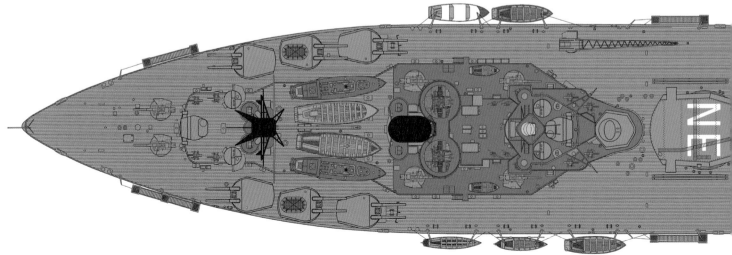

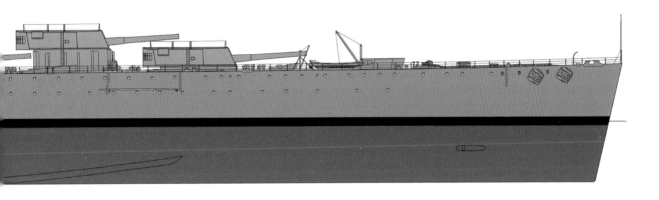

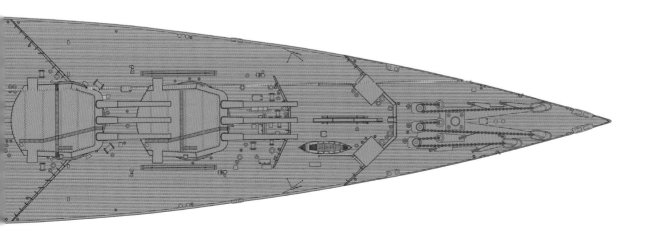

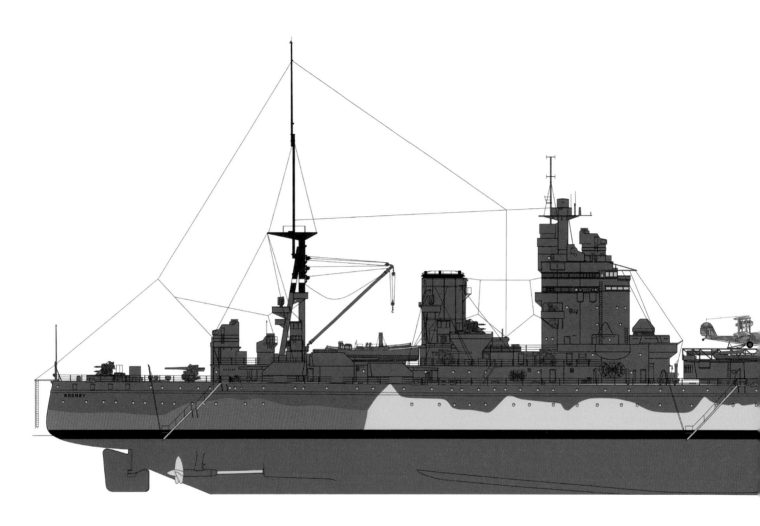

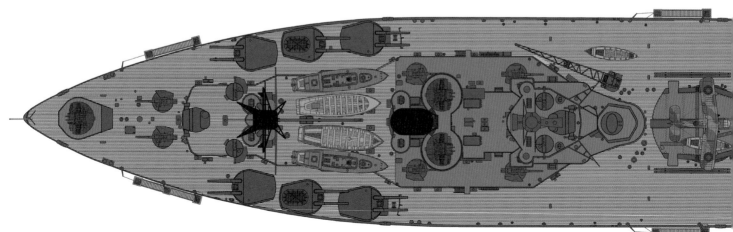

HMS Rodney *in 1940 paint scheme*

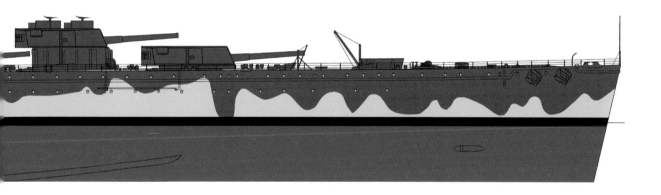

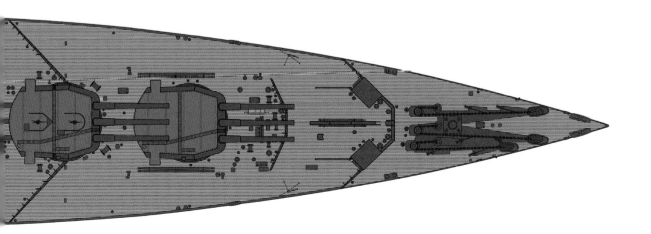

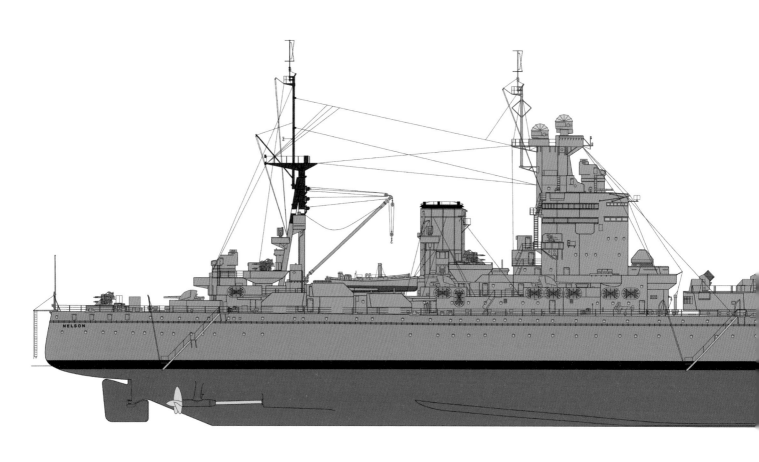

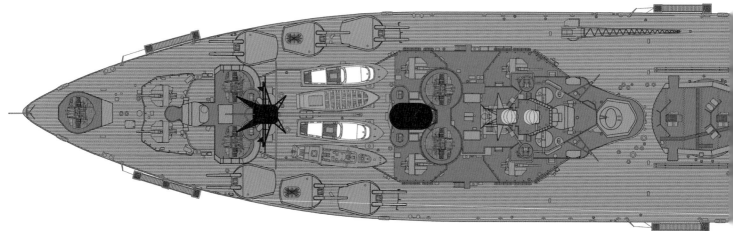

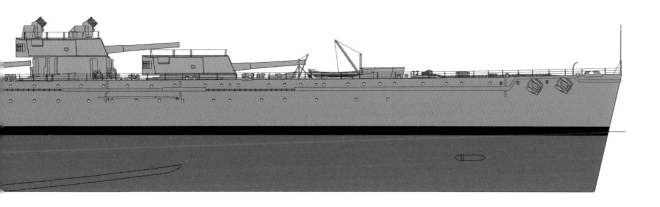

HMS Nelson *in 1940 paint scheme*

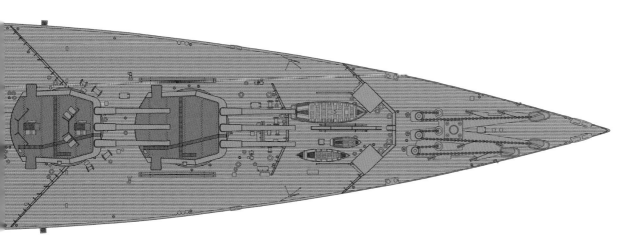

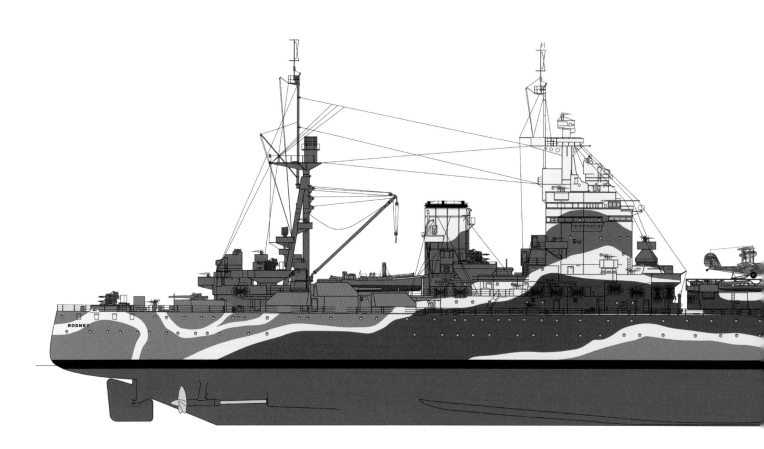

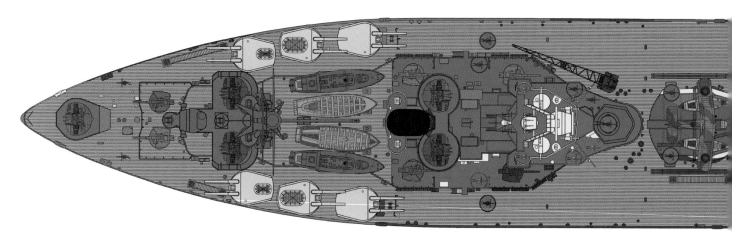

HMS Rodney *in 1942 paint scheme*

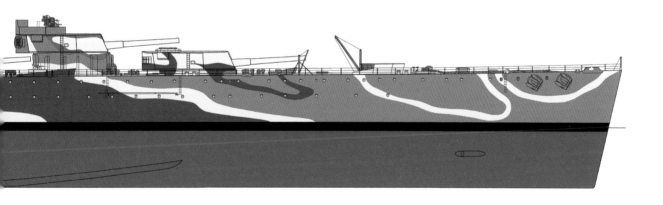

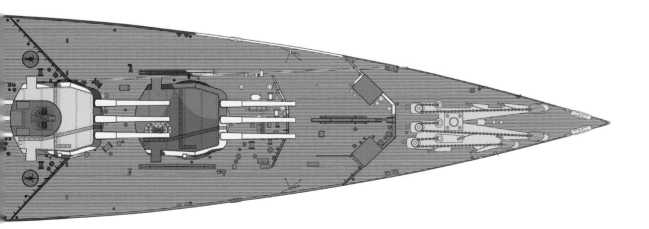

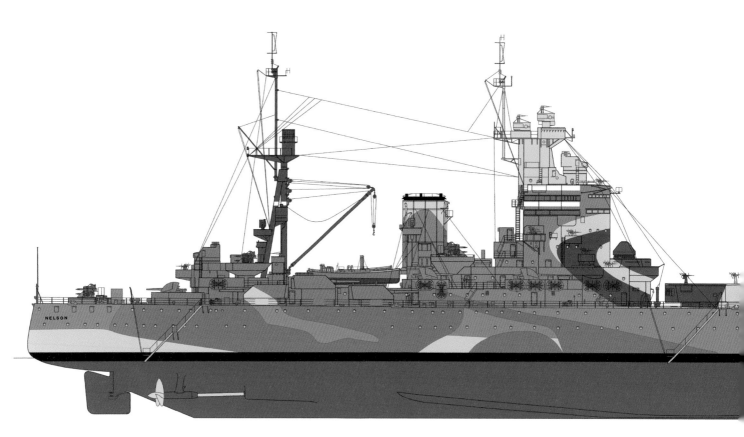

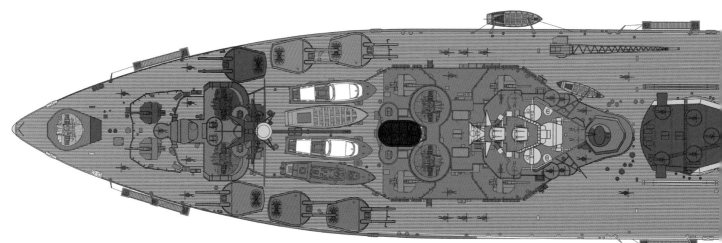

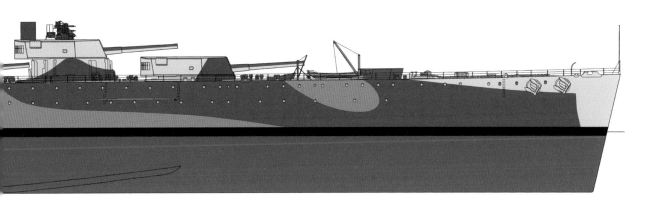

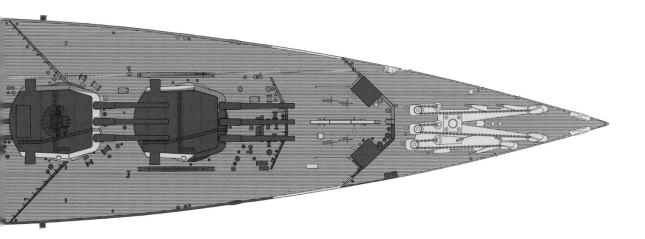

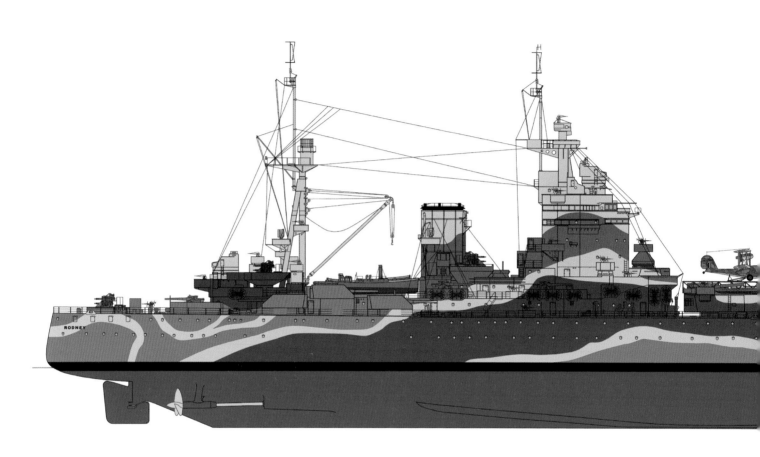

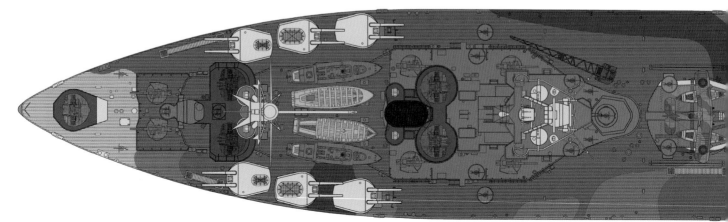

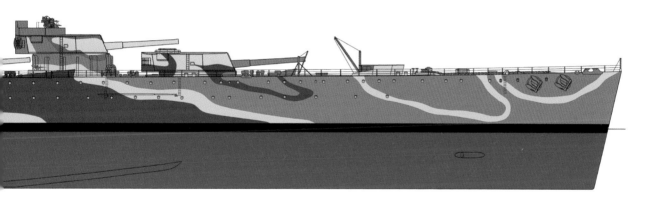

HMS Rodney *in 1943 paint scheme*

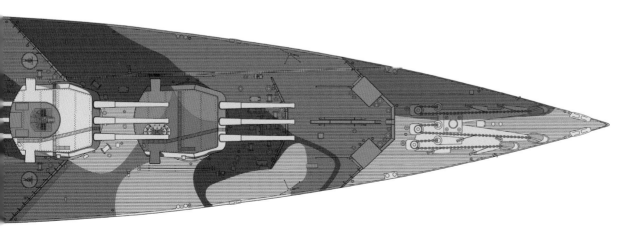

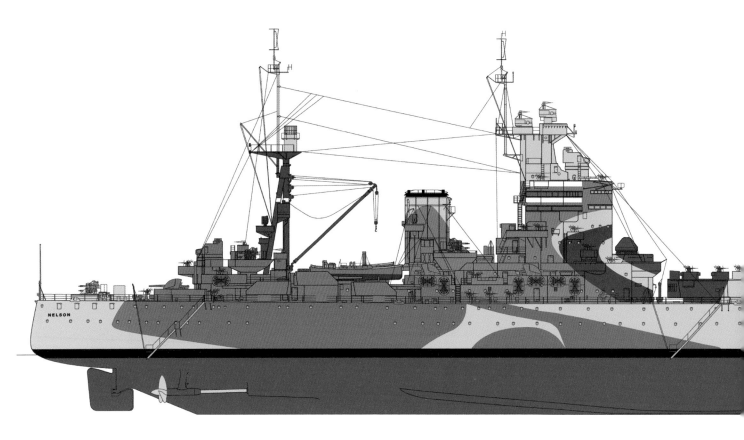

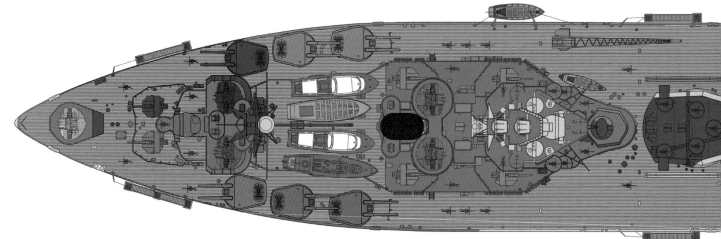

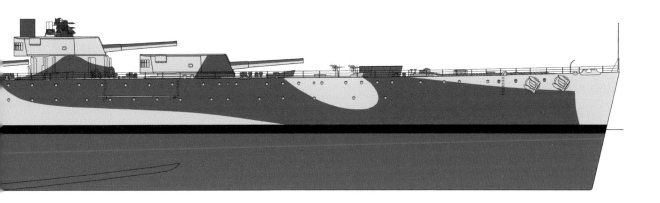

HMS Nelson *in 1943 paint scheme*

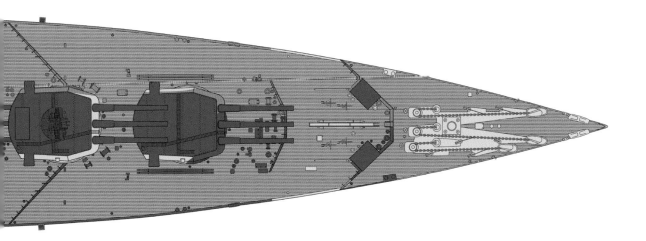

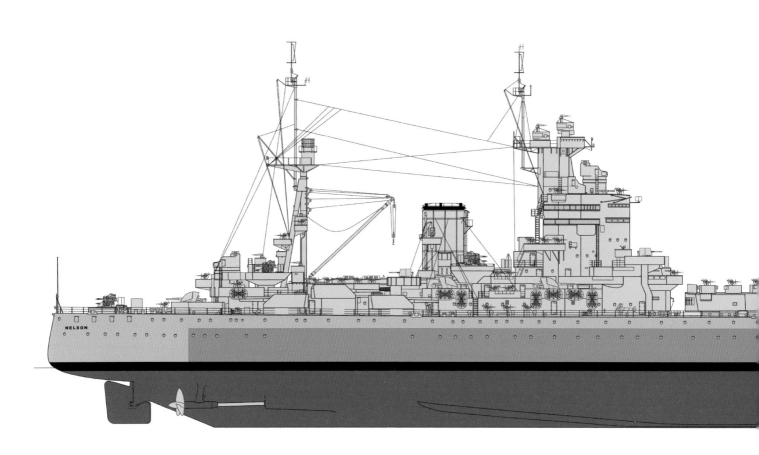

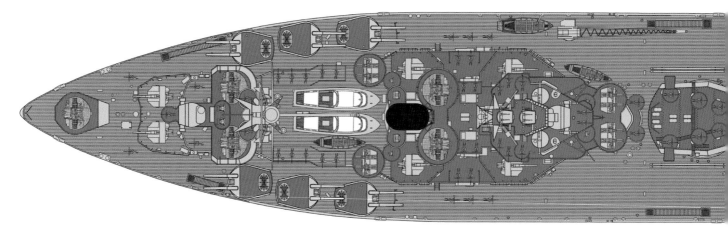

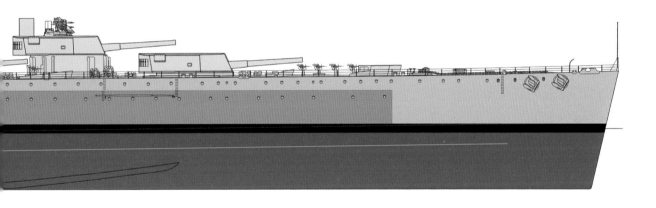

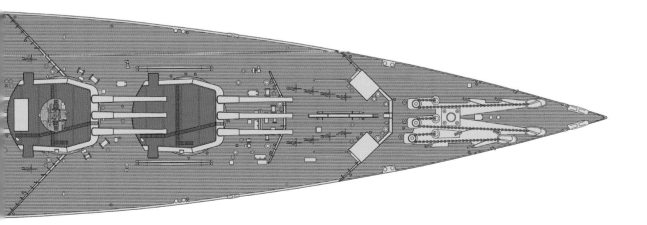